Kids at Hope:

Every Child Can Succeed, No Exceptions
*Dispelling the myth that kids are at risk.

John P. Carlos
Co-Author of the International Best Seller
Empowerment Takes More Than a Minute

Rick Miller
Founder, Kids at Hope

With Forewords by
Ken Blanchard
Co-Author of the One Minute Manager Book Series
&
Rosey Grier
Chairman, Impact Urban America
and Former NFL Great

Sagamore Publishing, LLC
804 N Neil
Champaign, IL 61822

http://www.sagamorepub.com

Library of Congress Catalog Card Number: 2009935100

ISBN:978-1-57167-577-4

Printed in the United States of America

Dedication

This book is dedicated to our grandchildren, who are
our Kids at Hope.

Madison Oleno
Megan Oleno
Kaitlyn Antunes
Delaney Antunes
Gabrielle Heredia
Jakob Emilio Heredia
Adrian Joaquin Magana-Miller

Special Dedication To:

Allan E. Miller,

my brother,
who each day demonstrates the power of hope

Foreword

by
Ken Blanchard

When John Carlos asked me to write the foreword for his book *Kids at Hope: Every Child Can Succeed, No Exceptions* co-authored by Rick Miller, I was thrilled for two reasons. First of all, I'm a big fan of John Carlos. The title on his business card sums it up. John calls himself "The Story Teller." He is one of the greatest teachers I know. He has always cared about the plight of kids. In fact, in the 20 years before we became friends, John had already worked with the Foundation for the Junior Blind as a coach for multi-handicapped blind children, for Rancho San Antonio "Boys Town of the West" as a counselor, and Saddle Club director and for three different member agencies of the Boys & Girls Clubs of America. So John is not only a great teacher, he is also one of the most caring human beings I know.

The second reason I am happy to write this foreword, is that I really think Kids at Hope could be the most important book written in the last decade to remedy the crisis of despair and lack of hope among our youth in America. I've known for a long time that the mind and the computer are similar in one way. They don't readily know the difference between the truth and what they are told.

If you put information in a computer, it doesn't ask, "Where did you get those figures? Those figures are wrong!" The computer does whatever it can with what you give it. For a long time, we've described the computer's ability to process information as "garbage in, garbage out." The same is true of the mind. The mind does not know the difference between the truth and what you tell it. If you get up in the morning, look in the mirror and say, "You are fabulous," your mind doesn't say, "Who are you kidding? I know better."

So, how we program kids' minds and what we put in is really important. I think John and Rick are really onto something. For a long time, we've talked about kids "at risk." What a self-fulfilling prophecy that is—whereas *Kids at Hope* is all about every child having the capacity to succeed, no exceptions.

Now, positive thinking isn't the only thing that's great about this book. I learned by working with Norman Vincent Peale on our book, *The Power of Ethical Management,* that when people read his classic book, *The Power of Positive Thinking,* sometimes they assumed all you had to have is positive thinking. Norman said, "That's not true. You also have to take some action. Just thinking positively isn't going to make you succeed." What do you do to succeed?

What's great about *Kids at Hope* are the tremendous ideas in here about what can be done in schools and communities to really create a culture of hope.

It's important that you hear the word "culture," because this book is not about establishing programs. Programs come and go, but if you can create a culture of hope, then everything that's done is done to help every kid succeed.

The big thing that Carlos and Miller emphasize is that everyone in our schools and the community, in the home and everywhere, should be responsible for kids' successes. These authors have great suggestions. In fact, they talk about the four aces that kids should have in their hands.

- Kids need anchor parents—parents who absolutely love them unconditionally and are there to support them.

- Kids need other caring adults (heroic figures)!

- Kids need high expectations and supportive adults who encourage kids to reach for goals that may, to the child, seem unattainable but are actually within reach.

- Kids also need opportunities to succeed.

So, read this book. Use this book! I believe it's the answer to empowering our kids to become the successful, happy adults they deserve to become.

Now, let me turn this foreword over to my friend and colleague, Rosey Grier. Rosey is a National Football League great, having played with the New York Giants, but he is best known as one of the Fearsome Foursome of the Los Angeles Rams. He has worked with the youth in this country relentlessly for over 30 years.

Recently, Rosey and I appeared before a U.S. Congressional committee that was looking into the drug situation in this country. Before we had a chance to speak, the senior congressman on the panel said, "I want to put it on the record that I am honored to be in the presence of Rosey Grier. A lot of people come and go around popular movements and ideas, but when that goes down, they're gone." He said, "Mr. Grier, you have devoted your life to supporting and encouraging and helping the youth, and I value that."

That's who Rosey Grier is. That's how much he cares about what John Carlos and Rick Miller are writing about.

Foreword

by
Rosey Grier

I love *Kids at Hope*. I think this is a fabulous book. When I first started traveling around the country into urban areas to help the youth, I was appalled by the run-down buildings I saw. In becoming familiar with those environments, I realized the buildings and apartments where people lived were not only run-down, but they were symptomatic of the lack of vision and hopelessness of the people. I concluded that when people change, the entire environment changes. Helping people change has been my quest for more than three decades. I want to make a difference for these young people, and so do John Carlos and Rick Miller.

One of the reasons I am excited about *Kids at Hope* is that not only are John and Rick trying to show people how to change kids' attitudes, but they are working on developing kids' skills and talents. This will enable kids to possess the tools necessary to make their lives more meaningful. When a person is prepared, and the opportunity presents itself, she or he is able to seize that opportunity and be productive.

Education is the molding force in preparing youth for their future endeavors. Creative teachers establish the atmosphere that is conducive for learning. Kids are motivated when the right atmosphere for learning is present. Singer BMX explains in a rap, "First, I'm going to crawl, then I'm going to walk, then I'm going to stand, then I'm going to talk, then I got to learn, then I'm gonna' teach, then I'm going to burn and I'm gonna reach." It's up to everyone involved in the lives of children to encourage kids to continue reaching.

Great attitudes and great skills will bring great success to everyone. Read *Kids at Hope*.

It is a continual challenge to set the stage for learning. Get your school and community involved in this important challenge to bring out the best we can in the young people of this country.

Table of Contents

Forewords 7, 11
Introduction.. 15
Background.. 19

Chapter One
The Visit Universal Truths I & II 24
Everyone has a different task at school, but we all share the same responsibility—to ensure the success of all our children, no exceptions.

Chapter Two
The Classroom (A Celebration of Success)...............38
We help our children succeed holistically.

Chapter Three
What Makes a Difference?...49
You must first reach a child before you can teach a child.

Chapter Four
No Exceptions! 57
For children to win the game of life, they need Aces. Adults control the Aces and must deal them to the children. The more Aces we deal children, the greater their chances of success.

Chapter Five
Defining Hope Universal Truth III...........................73
Life is not only a journey, it has destinations.

Chapter Six: Hope Square *(Hope²)* 84
A community that cares about its children must express such caring in everything and anything they do.

Chapter Seven: High Fives 91
When the future is all about children, then children must be all about the future.

Chapter Eight: Mr. Dawson Goes to Washington 97

Conclusion: From Parable to Reality
The Kids at Hope Story Continues
A Sampling of Case Studies from
Across the Country 100

Author Bios 119, 121

Introduction

Since its original publication in 2001, and revised editions in 2007 and again in 2009, *Kids at Hope* has truly captured the hopeful imagination of tens of thousands of caring adults across the country. Their belief in the potential of every young person has been restored and revalidated by this book. Each year, through one of our professional development seminars, institutes, classes, train the trainer events, books, videos, or keynote addresses, over 3,000 new "treasure hunters" from many walks of life are introduced to the Kids at Hope belief system and strategy.

Over the past several years, as we have established Kids at Hope models in communities, youth organizations, recreation sites, fire and police departments, and schools we have a much better understanding of the popular adage, "It takes a village to raise and educate a child." We know that statement is true, but it begs two questions: Who trains the village, and who in the village is invited to the training? Once you can articulate the question it makes it much easier to find the answer. We have learned that the capacity of Kids at Hope offers a model of training that reaches out to every adult, not because of their educational or professional status, but simply and most powerfully because of their interest in our youth.

You will discover through the adventures of our story protagonist, Robert Dawson, the Three Universal Truths and their High Five Practices that support a child's success. Robert Dawson learns that he must be able to see a future, which doesn't exist but is within reach. That has always, and will always be the only way we can shape our destiny. So, our basic question is, can we see a future where all children can succeed and there will not be any exceptions?

It hasn't been easy changing the paradigm and associated culture, which has taught us that many children are *at risk*, and therefore we shouldn't expect much from them. As a matter of fact, in one state in our union, planners look at second grade achievement scores as part of the formula they will need to determine how many prison cells they will require in the future. Talk about a self-fulfilling prophecy. I cannot imagine giving up on children in the second grade. I cannot imagine ever giving up on our kids. But whether we think we are or not, that is exactly what we do every day without even knowing it.

The youth *at-risk* label has prematurely judged our young people guilty until proven innocent. An entire industry has been created by the at-risk label. We have responded to the guilty verdict and its subsequent *at-risk* culture by ordering our youth to enter a series of prevention or intervention programs. For every pathology or potential pathology, we have created a separate program or activity to help children avoid negative and damaging behavior. Although laudable at first glance, these prevention programs have institutionalized the *at-risk* stereotype to the point where we have ignored our children's assets and strengths in order to focus on their problems and deficits. By doing so, we have unconsciously prohibited many children from achieving their unique scholastic, spiritual, social, and emotional potential.

Yet, in the face of these odds, Kids at Hope continues to make remarkable progress. I guess we are proving the renowned anthropologist Margaret Mead correct when she said, "Never doubt that a small group of thoughtful, committed citizens can change the world; indeed it's the only thing that ever has." I have come to respect and appreciate Dr. Mead's expression in action, and not just words. I wish I could say Kids at Hope had the uncompromising enthusiasm and leadership of many. We did not. What we did have was the commitment and shared vision of a few. And that was enough.

On behalf of all the children who have benefited from our efforts and who without question would have wallowed in the purgatory known as *at-risk* programs, I thank each and every one of you—you know who you are. I also thank those individuals and groups who are sharing their imagination in providing the intellectual, emotional, and financial capital needs to advance Kids at Hope.

I am quite excited about this third, newly revised edition of our book, *Kids at Hope: Every Child Can Succeed, No Exceptions*. This book, like our initiative, evolves each year. We are trying to keep pace with the experience and ongoing research associated with our initiative. We are equally excited to share our efforts with our colleagues in the fields of resiliency theory, research, and application as well as the maturing field of positive psychology. We continue to explore related disciplines in the fields of human services and education to ensure our principles and practices represent the best evidence available in support of the success of all children, without exception.

As with our previous editions, I am saddened by my co-author and dear friend John Carlos' sudden death in 2004 and that he is not with me to see this powerful initiative grow each year to a national and international initiative. John's spirit, however, is alive and strong in this book and the phenomenal message and action it offers in support of the success of all children, no exceptions!

Rick Miller
Founder and Chief Treasure Hunter
Kids at Hope

Background

In the early 1980s, the National Commission on Excellence in Education presented a study entitled "A Nation at Risk."

Its findings spawned an entire new culture and ultimate industry within our human services network by suggesting that many of America's children were "at risk." These children were threatened by a number of social and environmental factors that would seal their fate. They came from single-parent homes, or no-parent homes, were victims of child abuse or neglect, had parents who did not value education or were unable to speak the country's native tongue, lived in poverty, or were exposed to drugs, gangs, and related conditions. The more we studied these "at-risk" factors, the more "at-risk" factors we discovered. It wasn't long until many local and national leaders began to proclaim that many if not all America's children were "at risk."

With that, we heralded in a new era. Federal, state, and local governments, United Ways, foundations, and other funding sources challenged our service providers to retool their organizations to deal with these newly identified "at-risk" children. The more "at-risk" children you can identify, the more funds for which you would be eligible. It didn't take youth groups and education systems long before they could pronounce all children "at risk." It wasn't even necessary to look at children as individuals; we could make such a declaration once a neighbor or community was considered "at risk."

Yet, no one realized what the effect might be on the kids who were told they were "at risk." Did it occur to anyone that once a child hears that he or she is "at risk" to do something bad, chances are they'll believe it? And chances are, if they believe it, they'll eventually "be it." How about the adults who serve those children in the education or human services fields? Would the "at-risk" paradigm affect their conscious and unconscious beliefs and associated behaviors toward those children?

This notion implied that kids could not be trusted to be "at hope." In other words, it is wrong to assume that all kids want to be successful in life?

Or so they told us. Well, we personally had a hard time believing that kids woke up in the morning, looked in the mirror, and said to themselves, "Today, I will fail!"

"Supervise them closely, keep them busy, and always be on guard," we were told.

We were quick to identify the types of programs children would need that prevent them from the threats that swirled around them. If drugs were a problem, we directed our resources to drug prevention programs. Gangs? We created gang prevention programs. School drop outs? School drop-out prevention programs. Our creativity was limited to pilling on as many prevention or intervention programs as our imaginations could conceive. Our fundamental error was children don't grow up in programs or institutions; they grow up in communities. They are the sum total of all of their experiences, and yet we tried to divide and conquer these problems one at a time. Not only did we try to defeat these problems, we tried to do it by ignoring the "at-hope" factors that all of these children naturally possess.

So how have we been doing? Unfortunately, not so well. One only needs to look at our school achievement data or juvenile crime issues—gangs, drugs—or the number of children who just wander through life aimlessly to realize what we are doing isn't working well enough to help all children succeed.

So where do the answers lie? Well, not in focusing on our children's deficits or simply by creating one disconnected program after another.

Along with our colleagues in medicine, psychology, sociology, recreation, education, social work, and criminology, we began to look elsewhere for answers.

Albert Einstein changed the entire world of physics in the early 1900s by suggesting in his famous equation, $E=mc^2$, that energy and mass were different sides of the same coin. With that simple observation, he helped us more accurately understand our universe and how to harness its power.

What can we learn from Professor Einstein? For too long, we have only studied one side of the coin related to our children. We need to refocus our resources to a new science about our youth, one that would help us better understand and harness the hope side, the resiliency side, and the nature and nurture sides.

To achieve that purpose, we began to explore the new and emerging fields associated with human strengths, assets, brain research, and resiliency theory and application. We found fascinating research and cases studies in a wide range of disciplines. During a seven-year review, we began to identify not one study or another that seemed to underscore our understanding about how children succeed, even those who face many of life's greatest and horrific adversities, obstacles and challenges, but a series of the recurring themes that continued to appear throughout the disciplines we were exploring. The end result was our discovery of what we now reference as the *Three Universal Truths* needed to support the success of all children, without exception.

Subsequently, over an additional period of four years we learned about a series of five powerful and simple applications that would support the Three Universal Truths. We refer to those practices as our *High Fives.*

Our challenge was to identify a process and a format that would create not another new program on top of all the other new programs but to harness, as Einstein did, all the forces of the universe. We defined our universe as an organization, agency or community's culture. Our contribution was the development of a strategic cultural framework.

Furthermore, we wanted to establish a user-friendly understanding and protocol associated with the Three Universal Truths and its High Five Practices. Our goal was to make our findings available equally to any member of the culture/community, not just isolated to those who specialize in a program service or activity. It wasn't enough to empower human service or education administrators, social workers, psychologists, counselors, teachers, youth development workers, or other related professionals or para professionals.

If we were to truly harness the power of the universe/ culture, we need to include the not-so-usual suspects as well as the usual suspects we just referenced. What would happen if we invited the school bus drivers, custodial and food service staff, or front-office personnel, parents, and shopowners? What happens when the village is empowered to help all children succeed, without exception?

Our next challenge was how to present these *Three Universal Truths* and their *High Five Practices* in a manner that achieves our goal to empower an entire community and all the adults in the community who truly wish to believe in and support the success of all children.

Furthermore, we also wanted to validate those exceptional adults who chose not to buy into the *youth-at-risk* paradigm in spite of the misguided conventional wisdom of the day.

This book is one of many vehicles used in our efforts to share these remarkable truths and practices.

Therefore, you will find this book much different from other books that have done a wonderful job in sharing the new thinking and information related to resiliency, positive psychology, asset development, and brain research, all in an effort to help us advance our knowledge about children.

We chose to present our findings as a parable to demonstrate how we can bridge research with practice. By doing so, not only is the reader introduced to a series of profound, evidenced-based facts about youth, but he or she is also invited to enter the story where we have translated that data into a simple cultural framework at work every day in the City of Harrison.

Our findings are universal in their application. The story shared in this book is happening all over the country, including rural, urban and suburban communities.

At the end of this story, we have included a number of articles we have published in newspapers and magazines. It keeps our thinking fresh and our ability to share those insights with our readers.

We trust you will find our approach a unique and interesting way to learn about the emerging fields related to education as well as child and youth development and how this work can easily be used by an entire village with remarkable success.

One

The Visit
Universal Truths I & II

"WELCOME to Harrison, a Kids at Hope City, where the local time is 6:55 a.m.," came the announcement over the airplane's speakers as flight 236 taxied into its gate.

"A Kids at Hope City?" questioned Robert Dawson silently. "Is that what the flight attendant said?"

Robert gathered his personal belongings, and as he approached the plane's door, he stopped for a moment to speak to the flight attendant.

"Did you say something about a Kids at Hope City?" queried Robert.

"Yes, sir," the polite attendant responded, "Harrison is a Kids at Hope City."

"What is a Kids at Hope City?" asked Robert.

"Simply speaking, it's a community . . . ," the flight attendant was interrupted by a gate agent who apparently had an emergency. "Sorry, got to go," the attendant apologized and quickly disappeared into the jet way.

Robert's interest was piqued, but he had an appointment he needed to rush to, so off he went to claim his baggage. As he boarded the downward escalator, he noticed an illuminated display sign advertising, "Welcome to Harrison, A Kids at Hope City." At the bottom right of the sign appeared the city logo that read, "Incorporated 1926." On the left side of the sign was a sunburst logo with three starlike characters that read. "Kids at Hope No Exceptions!"

"Interesting," was Robert's immediate thought. He believed this intriguing secret would soon be revealed.

After picking up his checked bags and rental car, Robert headed off to his 9 a.m. appointment with Mildred Ramirez, principal of Lincoln Elementary School.

It was 8:15 a.m., and traffic was unusually lighter than he had expected. He arrived for his appointment much earlier than scheduled.

The extra 45 minutes was a welcomed luxury. Robert normally ran late for his meetings, but not this time. Robert had a moment to catch his breath before his customary busy day. He seemed to truly enjoy the fact that life had slowed down, and instead of feeling like a hostage of time, he began to observe the rhythm of students, teachers, and staff preparing for another school day. He headed toward the school office.

"Sometimes you miss a lot of important things when you are so busy being busy," he mused.

"Stop and smell the roses," he remembered his wife telling him. And for a moment, he was "smelling the roses."

A school bus stopped about 30 feet from where Robert was standing. Robert watched as the students disembarked. Curiously, the bus driver caught Robert's eye.

As each child left the bus, Robert overheard the driver encouraging the children. "Do your best today. I'm proud of you," he said to every boy and girl, looking each one directly in the eye. A few students actually stopped and whispered something in the driver's ear. Each comment was exchanged for a smile and off the children ran to their classrooms.

When the bus was emptied, a young woman ran over to the driver and slipped him a note.

Robert was surprised by the unusual interactions he was witnessing. Robert decided to approach the bus driver.

"Hi, and excuse me," Robert said, as he extended his hand to the driver. "My name is Robert Dawson, and I'm visiting from the U.S. Department of Education."

"Hello, my kids call me 'Chief,'" responded the bus driver, as he shook Robert's hand.

"I couldn't help but notice how you interacted with each of the students from your bus," Robert offered. "I mean, you seemed to genuinely express interest in each and every one of them."

"Well, they're my kids," Chief proudly noted. "I know what you are thinking. Bus drivers drive buses, teachers teach, and administrators administer."

"I guess that is what I'm getting at," Robert said.

"Not here," Chief said. "At our school, we are all responsible for our kids."

"Could you please explain what you mean by that?" Robert politely asked.

"Sure. When I applied for this job, I filled out a regular application. You know, name, address, and experience, the whole ball of wax. But when I was interviewed, everything was a bit unusual."

"I'm not quite following you," Robert said.

"Well, in my previous bus-driving jobs, I am normally interviewed by the director of transportation or a high-level supervisor. The questions are usually the same. But this interview was anything but normal. First, the committee was made up of the principal, a teacher, parents, and the transportation supervisor. They all interviewed me. They asked me questions about how driving a bus could help a student succeed in school. I confess that question floored me. Why would they be asking me that type of question? After all, I wasn't applying as a teacher. I just wanted to be a bus driver. It's not rocket science, you know?" Chief said.

Robert asked, "What happened?"

"Well, the interview committee said, 'All our employees must focus on the end result ... the success of all our kids,'" Chief answered.

"The committee then asked me to complete a one-question survey," added the Chief.

Chief described a survey that asked, *"Do you believe all children are capable of success, no exceptions?"*

On a scale from "1" to "10," with the number one representing strongly disbelieve or disagree with that statement and the number ten representing strongly believe or agree with the statement. Numbers from 2-9 are degrees from strongly disbelieve/disagree to strongly believe/ agree.

"Fascinating," responded Robert.

The school district refers to that survey as the *World's Most Important Question.*

"We ask everyone that question who applies for a job with our district," stated Chief.

Robert learned that the district had commissioned a study to better understand why some children, especially those who face seemingly insurmountable obstacles, adversities, and challenges in life still seem to succeed, while many others who had all the advantages appeared to struggle. The district learned that conventional wisdom of the past that supported the belief that children from poverty, homes with neglectful or even abusive parents, high incidence of drugs and gangs, parents who performed poorly in school were illiterate, or who could not speak or write in the language of the country they live, were "at risk," of failing educationally, socially, emotionally, and economically.

The district's research revealed three powerful findings that have transformed the school culture from one "at risk" to one "at hope." Those findings are now referred to as the "Three Universal Truths," because they appear throughout the scientific literature including medicine, sociology, psychology, social work, education, recreation, and criminology. In other words, the district was focusing on the success factors that all children need rather than obsessing over the "at-risk" excuses that have been refuted.

The first of the powerful Universal Truths state that:

> **Universal Truth #1:**
> *Children succeed when they are surrounded by adults who believe they can succeed, without exception.*

Armed with that first finding/universal truth, the district needed to know whether they were surrounding children with adults who believed that *all children are capable of success and there are no exceptions*, regardless of the student's environmental or personal conditions.

"I get it," noted Robert, "If adults don't believe that all children can succeed, they may unconsciously support a student's failure."

"That's it!" answered Chief. "And unfortunately, they won't even know it."

Robert remembered studying the *Pygmalion Effect* from his college days. A landmark study that proved that teachers' impressions of children, whether those assessments are accurate or not, impact students' achievements, good and bad. He hadn't thought much about that study since his undergraduate days, but it appears to still make sense.

"What happens when an applicant chooses a number other than ten?" questioned Robert.

"That becomes problematic," answered a voice from behind Robert.

It was the woman who earlier slipped Chief, the bus driver, a note.

Robert turned around and was introduced to Ms. Thomas, a fifth grade teacher at Lincoln Elementary School.

Ms. Thomas added that if applicants or even current teachers, administrators, or staff can't choose "10" they, not the students or their parents or even their social circumstances, may unwittingly be placing students "at risk."

"That really does shed a whole new way of thinking about our children," concluded Robert.

Ms. Thomas noted that when the school first introduced the *World's Most Important Question*, the average score was certainly less than ten.

"We weren't surprised by our findings," continued Ms. Thomas. "We understood that for much too long we have offered our faculty and staff wrong information about success and failure. We bought into the 'at-risk' paradigm and gave up on too many children, especially those children who really needed someone to believe they could make it despite their circumstances."

Chief nodded approvingly, agreeing with Ms. Thomas' assessment.

Since the *World's Most Important Question* was introduced, the district now understands how important it is to its students to hire people who can choose number 10. The district also supports professional development experiences that focus on the body of research that validates the importance of an adult's belief in children.

"Our people need to know as do their parents and community, the power of our beliefs in children . . . all children," re-emphasized Ms. Thomas.

"Hey, I have to run, I have to get to my class," a hurried Ms. Thomas, just realized. "Hope to catch you later."

"Before you leave, can you tell me about the note you left with Chief?" asked Robert.

"I was letting Chief know that one of my students was improving nicely, and I suggested he comment about it when he next sees her," responded Ms. Thomas.

With that, Ms. Thomas disappeared as quickly as she had appeared a few moments earlier.

Robert and Chief continued their conversation.

"Do you know what my title is?" Chief asked Robert.

"School bus driver, I assume," Robert responded.

"You're half right," Chief said. "It's bus driver and treasure hunter. Sorry to cut this short, but I have a field trip I need to prepare for," noted Chief. "Nice meeting you."

"Same here," said Robert.

As Chief boarded his bus and drove off, Robert glanced at the back of the bus where that same *Kids at Hope* logo appeared. **NO EXCEPTIONS** it boldly read.

Treasure Hunter: A caring adult who searches beneath the surface to find all the talents, skills, and intelligence that exist in children.

"May I help you?" asked a friendly voice from behind the counter in the school's office.

"Hello, I'm Robert Dawson, and I have a 9 a.m. appointment with Mrs. Ramirez."

"Welcome to Lincoln Elementary, a Kids at Hope School," offered Esther Disen, school secretary.

"Hmmm," Robert thought to himself. "A Kids at Hope School, a Kids at Hope City, a Kids at Hope bus, a Treasure Hunter and the *World's Most Important Question* . . . Hmmm."

The secretary just smiled at Robert as he was quietly contemplating his thoughts.

"Please be seated, Mr. Dawson. I'll let Mrs Ramirez know that you are here," the school secretary said.

As he waited two students, a boy and a girl, ran up to the counter.

"You made it!" the secretary noted, "Good for you. Here is a *Glad You Made It* pass. Now hurry up!"

Robert was somewhat taken aback by what he had just seen. Two students who were obviously late would normally get a little scolding and a late pass to get them into class. But that is not what he observed.

"Excuse me . . . may I ask you a question?" Robert asked the secretary.

"Indeed," was her response.

"Those two students were late, but you seemed to dismiss their tardiness," reported Robert.

"Well, it's not that simple," answered the secretary. "Lots of our students face some real hardships getting to school. Like most schools, we frown upon tardiness, but we learned in many cases not to blame the children, especially those children we know are embarrassed by their lateness.

"Often it's not their fault. So, as part of our Kids at Hope culture, we celebrate attendance, knowing that many of our children make a great and sincere effort to get to school even under difficult circumstances."

Robert thought about the secretary's answer for a few moments. *Glad You Made It* instead of a tardy slip? This was the school's effort to catch kids doing things right, and for many of them, getting to school was the right thing to do in spite of the hardships in their lives.

Robert discovered that for many years, the school had had a poor attendance history. Instead of looking for blame, they sought solutions. One answer was to encourage good attendance by limiting the negative attention offered to tardiness and replacing it with positive recognition for making it to school.

"This Kids at Hope school thing is getting more and more curious," thought Robert.

Robert thanked the secretary for her explanation.

"Incidentally," she noted, "You know I am also a Treasure Hunter."

A second later, two more children entered the office. They appeared to be brother and sister, and both were returning from a doctor's appointment. "Now, quickly, before I give you your pass, tell me about something you succeeded in yesterday," the secretary/treasure hunter requested.

Robert, listening to the conversation, found the question unusual. However, the girl, whom he believed to be eight years old, blurted out, "I won the spelling bee yesterday!"

"Good for you, Leah," complimented the secretary. "How about you, Torry?" she asked.

Torry looked about six or seven years old.

"I don't know," was Torry's timid response.

"What do you mean, you don't know? In our school everyone succeeds every day, somehow and somewhere," the secretary encouraged.

"Not Torry," his sister piped in. "He didn't do so well on his writing project yesterday."

"I'm sure he'll do better next time. Right, Torry?" asked the secretary. "Although grades are very important, they are not the only way to measure success. Can't you think of something you did well yesterday, Torry?" the secretary persisted.

"I helped my mom with the dishes, and she said I did a good job," Torry recalled.

"That's good! That's good!" responded the secretary. "There are lots of ways to be successful, and they are all important. Good job, Torry and good job, Leah! I'm proud of the two of you. Now get to class, pronto!"

Soon after the children ran out of the office, Mildred Ramirez, the school principal, greeted Robert.

"I'm sorry I made you wait, Mr. Dawson. Welcome to our Kids at Hope school," Mrs. Ramirez said.

"It's no problem. I've really enjoyed watching your staff interact with the students," he said.

"Would you like something to drink, Mr. Dawson?" Mrs. Ramirez asked.

"A cup of coffee would work," Robert said.

"Coming up," responded Mrs. Ramirez. "So, what brings you all the way from Washington, D.C.?" she asked.

"I'm preparing a report for the Secretary of Education about exemplary school programs, and your school was recommended for observation," Robert answered.

"I'm flattered, Mr. Dawson. What would you like to know?" Mrs. Ramirez asked.

Before addressing his formal questions, Robert was anxious to know more about what he had seen earlier.

"When our plane landed this morning, the flight attendant welcomed us to Harrison, 'A Kids at Hope City,'" stated Dawson. "There was a sign at the airport also welcoming us to a Kids at Hope City. I then saw the Kids at Hope logo on one of your buses, and both you and your secretary refer to Lincoln Elementary as a Kids at Hope school. So what's the story behind the story?" asked Robert.

"Well, let me try to explain," offered Mrs. Ramirez.

"About seven years ago, this school was having a lot of problems. Performance was low, behavioral problems were high, morale was low, and teacher turnover was high. We needed to take some action—and fast—or we were headed for real disaster."

"What did you do?" Robert asked.

"Well, first our district commissioned a study about why some kids succeed regardless of the adversity they experience, and others don't," described Mrs. Ramirez.

"Yes, I learned a little about that earlier this morning," responded Robert.

"Then you know about our belief system, that all children are capable of success, No Exceptions.

"I'm beginning to," stated Robert.

"Well, let me add a little more background to how we got here," continued Mrs. Ramirez.

"We realized that the job of educating our children was not just the responsibility of the school and its teachers, but that the entire community had a role in the success of our children. Our quality of life is directly tied to our students' success. We also realized that the school's responsibility was to set the tone for the rest of the community. In other words, if we didn't believe that all our children could succeed and act like we believe that, we couldn't create the culture we now understood was required on behalf of all children. We needed to create a culture where we could select ten on the *World's Most Important Question*. So, we began by redefining all of our roles in terms of the end result. For example, 'success' rather than 'job descriptions,'" Mrs. Ramirez said. "We then engaged our entire city in a remarkable experiment."

"Why don't I give you a tour? It's easier to understand if you see it in action," Mrs. Ramirez suggested.

As Mrs. Ramirez and Roger Dawson left for their tour of the campus, Mr. Dawson asked about the Three Universal Truths that were revealed in the school district's study.

"That study got all of us on the same page," responded Mrs. Ramirez. "I understand you have already been introduced to Universal Truth One, which states that *children succeed when they are surrounded by adults who believe they can succeed.* Our school added *No Exceptions* to that finding. Let me tell you about Universal Truth Two."

Mrs. Ramirez's voice increased in pace and volume, as she was obviously excited to share information about the second Universal Truth.

"The study's second most profound finding was that "Children succeed when they have meaningful and sustainable relationships with caring adults," offered Mrs. Ramirez. "Although that finding, like Universal Truth number one, seems so obvious, its practice is not as apparent.

"What do you mean?" asked Mr. Dawson.

Mrs. Ramirez explained that as part of its efforts to understand the implications of each of the Universal Truths, it had to collect baseline data. In the case of Universal Truth number two, the district had to determine whether or not its students were experiencing meaningful and sustainable relationships with caring adults. According to Mrs. Ramirez, the results were not too encouraging.

"Our study discovered that 20 percent of our students were not connected by a meaningful and sustainable relationship with a caring adult. Talk about a wake-up call. . . ." stated Mrs. Ramirez. "If we are trying to help children succeed, we need to connect with them, and that wasn't happening. Growing up disconnected from adults removes a needed buffer from the threats that exist in any young person's life.

"So what did you do?" asked Mr. Dawson.

"A whole lot," answered Mrs. Ramirez. "I'll tell you more after we visit Mrs. Rashad's class.

Universal Truth #2:
*Children succeed when they have meaningful
and sustainable relationships with caring adults.*

Dawson's Reflection:

There was a "Chief" in my life. It was in the third grade, but he was not a bus driver. He was the school janitor, but neither I nor any of my classmates ever thought of him as the janitor. He was "Ed." Ed always had kind words. I can still hear his Irish brogue saying, "Top 'o the mornin' to everyone." I remember him sharing his lunch and his time with us. He always offered to help us clean up our mess at the lunch table. He had this old army jeep. We thought it was so cool. I wonder now if Ed wasn't really a teacher in disguise.

Everyone is a teacher, huh? Why does that make me think of my vacation in Ireland? Ah, yes, the boomerang. I remember now. It was a supermarket, SuperQuinn.

When we entered the market, the first thing my wife said was, "How strange. The employee name tags are shaped like miniature boomerangs."

I thought, "Boomerangs don't belong in Ireland. They belong in Australia."

I approached the man at the meat counter and asked, "What's with the boomerang?"

The man smiled and replied, "Well, what does a boomerang do when you throw it?"

I answered, "It comes back."

He said, "That's our job, to make you want to come back. Our jobs aren't just cutting meat, stocking bags, operating the till, or doing maintenance. Those are our individual tasks, but our job is the same. And that is, to make sure you come back. Cutting meat is just a task, something I do. What I am accountable for is the experience you have in our store. What can I do to make you want to come back?"

Interesting, why didn't I see these connections before? What can the schools do to make children want to be there?

Two

The Classroom:
A Celebration of Success

MRS. RAMIREZ and Robert entered Mrs. Alicia Rashad's fifth-grade classroom as quietly as possible to avoid disrupting the class. Within a split second, however, all the heads in the class turned to look at the two visitors.

"Please excuse the interruption," Mrs. Ramirez said.

"Welcome," returned Mrs. Rashad.

Mrs. Ramirez introduced Robert Dawson, "This is our guest, Mr. Dawson. He is visiting from the United States Department of Education."

A murmur spread through the classroom. The students looked at Robert and determined that he was a very important person.

"Please continue," encouraged Mrs. Ramirez. "We will be extremely quiet."

"Martha, will you please lead the class in the Pledge of Allegiance?" requested Mrs. Rashad.

The class joined Martha in the recitation of the Pledge.

"And Jake, will you please lead the class in the Kids at Hope Pledge?" invited Mrs. Rashad.

"Kids at Hope Pledge?" Robert wondered.

The class joined Jake in reciting the following:

I am a Kid at Hope.
I am talented, smart, and capable of success.
I have dreams for the future,
and I will climb to reach my goals
and dreams every day.
All children are capable of success,
No Exceptions!

"Never heard that one," Robert thought.

As Robert was digesting what he just heard, his eyes began to dart from student to student. Something was different, but he couldn't quite place it. Then it became clear. Every student was wearing a T-shirt representing a college or university.

Mrs. Ramirez was watching Robert carefully, trying to read his expressions as he was introduced to a series of new concepts.

All eyes returned to Mrs. Rashad after the class recited the Kids at Hope pledge.

"What's today?" she then asked.

"Report card day," cheered the class.

"You are correct," Mrs. Rashad exclaimed.

Each student appeared excited to receive a report card. The children were completely focused on the stack of cards Mrs. Rashad was holding in her hand.

She called each student's name, and one by one, the children eagerly approached Mrs. Rashad to receive their report cards. When they returned to their desks, they anxiously opened their cards and read what their teacher had written. Most students giggled at the results. All had genuine smiles on their faces.

"Funny," Robert thought. He had witnessed this custom for many, many years. He remembered his own experience as a young student. It was a day of celebration for some,

REPORT CARD

COMMUNITY &
SERVICE

HOME &
FAMILY

HOBBIES &
RECREATION

EDUCATION &
CAREER

ALL KIDS ARE CAPABLE
OF SUCCESS,

NO EXCEPTIONS!

disappointment for others, and as expected for everyone else. But within this classroom, it was a big celebration.

After allowing the students time to absorb the information she had given, Mrs. Rashad kindly asked the class to settle down.

"I'm so proud of each of you," Mrs. Rashad said. "I am so very proud of you," she repeated.

The students giggled and applauded. Most importantly, they were happy with their achievements.

"Report Card Day," Robert reflected, "seems more like the last day of school."

"Time to go," Mrs. Ramirez said.

"Ah, OK, sure," Robert acknowledged.

Mrs. Ramirez and Robert walked into an empty hallway. Classes were in session, and the corridor was quiet.

"So, did you see or hear anything interesting?" Mrs. Ramirez asked.

"Yes, quite interesting," Robert replied.

"Well?" questioned Mrs. Ramirez.

"Well, when we first walked in and the students recited the Pledge of Allegiance, I assumed it was the start of a typical school day. But they then recited another oath that caught me completely off guard," Robert noted.

"What was that oath called again?" Robert asked.

"That's our Kids at Hope Pledge," answered Mrs. Ramirez.

"Kids at Hope Pledge?" Robert repeated. "What does it all mean?"

"It's a simple affirmation to support our belief system that every child can succeed, no exceptions!" offered Mrs. Ramirez. "If we believe it about our students, they need to believe it as well. They need to be able to say the words, hear the words, and most importantly, understand and practice the words.

"I know what you are thinking," offered Mrs. Ramirez.

"You do?" asked Robert.

"Yes, you think the oath may be too simple and possibly trite," continued Mrs. Ramirez.

"Well, it did cross my mind," responded a surprised Robert.

"Well, it is simple, but it is also enormously powerful," answered Mrs. Ramirez. "But don't underestimate the simple but powerful message that it offers, which becomes part of our overall culture."

During the district's study, the concept of *positive self-talk* was explored. It became clear that students, and for that matter, even adults who learn about *positive self-talk* and practice its principles live more successful lives than people who don't. Once the district understood that finding, it made all the sense in the world to help children learn and practice the value of *positive self-talk.*

"This may be the dumb question of the day, but why do you use the term *Kids at Hope?*" Robert asked.

"Because it is the opposite of that which we have believed and accepted for much too long, and that is that our children are *at risk.* They aren't *at risk,* and we have popularized that expression to the detriment of recognizing the *hope* that lies in all our children!" offered Mrs. Ramirez. "Our students and all children are in fact at hope.

"We will learn more about that later," concluded Mrs. Ramirez. "Was there anything else that you noticed?" she asked.

"The kids were all in college T-shirts or sweatshirts," observed Robert.

"Yes, the T-shirts," acknowledged Mrs. Ramirez, "They are also part of our belief system and culture. Education is a lifelong experience. As we establish our Kids at Hope culture, we need to make sure we are representing our beliefs in language, behavior, traditions, signs, artifacts . . . all the components that symbolize a culture. We want all our students to know, in no uncertain terms, that we believe in them and we wish to encourage them to pursue higher education. Keeping the high bar high is important, and in doing so, we create a culture that supports that belief. Having children wear college-emblazoned shirts, at least once a quarter, is a simple way to reinforce that belief. Sometimes our teachers invite our alumni to talk about their college experiences. We want our children to see these former students as role models. We want them to understand that college is an option for everyone. In fact, one of the home-work assignments we give our older students is to prepare a paper on the college or post secondary schools of their choice, usually reflected by the T-shirts they wear. We ask them to present their findings to the class. We want them to know that education in its many different expressions is one major key to success."

"I've never thought about it before, but I hear what you are saying. If you believe that all your children are capable of success, you will treat them that way," offered Robert. "I remember that my brother and sister-in-law dressed their newborn in a baby T-shirt representing the college they attended. I guess they were already establishing a belief that my nephew would go to college. It was an early expectation."

"That's right," reinforced Mrs. Ramirez. "We realize that most children who go to college have that goal instilled in them at an early age. It's something you do when you grow up. We, therefore, create a culture that supports our belief that all children can succeed. There is also one more major concept we instill in our students."

"What's that?" Robert inquired.

"Our students know their graduation dates," Mrs. Ramirez proudly stated.

"High school graduation?" Robert questioned.

"No, all our children know their college or post secondary graduation dates," Mrs. Ramirez informed her surprised guest.

"Every one?" a surprised Robert asked.

"Every one," answered a proud Mrs. Ramirez. "Kindergartners through our eighth graders all know and have always known what date they will be graduating from college or the post secondary school of their choice. Remember, our culture is about high expectations and NO EXCEPTIONS!

"Reminding our students about our high expectations for them shows we believe they are all capable of achieving that goal. Having caring adults support that expectation and creating the opportunities to ensure such achievement, is what we should always be about," she continued.

"That all makes great sense," Robert stated." I must also confess that I wasn't sure about the report card scene. Can you tell me something about it?"

"Yes, the report card scene. Very interesting, don't you think?" asked Mrs. Ramirez. Mrs. Ramirez spoke to Mr. Dawson about her concern as well as those shared by many of her parents that too much emphasis was being placed on grades and test scores, which only measures behavior and places little, if any, importance on potential. At Lincoln School, everyone knows the importance placed on grades, but it doesn't exclude the recognition and need to share information about our students' potential."

Mr. Dawson liked the concept, but like so many others, determined that there was not any way one could measure potential. Mrs. Ramirez again emphasized the value of treasure hunting.

"You see," offered Mrs. Ramirez, "treasure hunting is all about looking beyond the behavior to identify the potential in children. Treasure hunters use the Kids at Hope report card as one of the tools needed to go beyond test scores and grades. It helps to focus on a student's nonacademic talent, skills, characteristics, and traits. If we can identify those attributes, expose and develop them, great positive results will be achieved, academically, emotionally, and socially. It is incumbent on adults to do so."

"Our Kids at Hope report card," continued Mrs. Ramirez, "recognizes that although reading, writing, and math are critically important in life, you need additional skills, talents, and intelligence to succeed. It's a report card that recognizes that success is not just a score or a grade in a subject matter. It's about what we call *total success*."

"Total success?" Robert asked.

"You see, Mr. Dawson, the reason for education is to help children succeed in life. But first you must define success. If we can't define success, then all we are doing in school is offering a set of classes, subjects, and programs without clearly and dramatically defining their value to the elusive term we call success," explained Mrs. Ramirez.

"So, how do you define success?" Robert asked.

"Totally and holistically. In other words, we realize that success isn't some*thing*, but some*where*. In other words, we learned that success is the capacity and expectation that we will contribute to a series of destinations where life's journey will take us to. The journey includes our ability to contribute to those destinations including our home and family life, education and career, community and service, and hobbies and recreation.

"This is where life's journey is going to take you. So you see, life is about succeeding at all four destinations," Mrs. Ramirez went on.

"Wait a second," interrupted Robert. "Don't you believe that 'life is a journey, not a destination?'"

"I used to," responded Mrs. Ramirez, "until we began to explore the word success. It had different meanings to different people. We needed a common definition so our students wouldn't be confused. Our research helped us frame the word success.

"The district understood it was preparing students to be lifelong learners. It was preparing students to understand that success is the ability to contribute at life's four major destinations. Therefore, the important question is: what are the skills, talents, characteristics, and intelligence needed to succeed at each of life's destination points?

"The report card helps identify the talents, skills, characteristics, and intelligence required for success at life's four destinations. The Kids at Hope report card also underscores that which we understand about our children. We believe each child is unlike any other person. Their uniqueness is their strength. We shouldn't steal that from them."

Robert Dawson learned the report cards honor each child's individuality and offers them insight about their talents. The report card demonstrates the use of those strengths and assets in the real world. For example, is kindness and creativity of equal value with reading and math? The reality is, it is! But one doesn't substitute for the other. They are both needed. Therefore, the reason students get excited about the report card is it celebrates their uniqueness and the future value they possess.

"So what you are saying is there are many ways to be smart?" Robert offered.

"Yes, indeed," answered Mrs. Ramirez. "How do you define 'smart,' Mr. Dawson?" continued Mrs. Ramirez.

"That's a good question," replied Robert, "Let me toss that question back to you, as I suspect you have a pretty good answer."

"Yes, I do," offered Mrs. Ramirez. "Try this as a definition: 'Smart is what the world needs and what you have.'"

"Very interesting," Robert responded. "What the world needs, huh? Well . . . well, the world needs good doctors, but it also needs honest people. And the world needs engineers, but it also needs compassionate people. Is that the gist?"

"Yes, sir," replied Mrs. Ramirez. "And our students need to understand that concept. And the only way we can ensure we are preparing all students for the challenges that await them in their futures is to create a culture of treasure hunters."

The Harrison Unified School District promotes the importance of treasure hunting as part of its culture. The superintendent is a treasure hunter as are the bus drivers. Police officers are treasure hunters, and parents learn about the tools of treasure hunting.

Robert Dawson began to understand and appreciate the power of the Kids at Hope report card and the concept of treasure hunting. He recognized that in most schools, students are judged on behavior, but in a Kids at Hope school, one day is set aside where you can't fail. It's also a day when students can understand how their unique strengths and talents are related to their futures. Everyone needs such a day in their lives. Mrs. Ramirez's school guarantees it.

"What is your title again, Mr. Dawson?" Mrs. Ramirez asked Robert.

"Director of Programs," he replied. "Oh, and a Treasure Hunter, I guess," Robert said.

"That is absolutely correct," Mrs. Ramirez said happily. "A culture that values children doesn't just define its role in terms of tasks—which appear on a business card— but also in terms of their shared responsibility—which is what we represent to children as adults. A culture in which adults accept their primary shared responsibility as treasure hunters sets the stage for all children to succeed," she explained.

Dawson's Reflection:

This reminds me of a seminar I attended years ago called "Succeeding at Your Moment of Truth." Jan Carlzon, president of Scandinavian Airlines (SAS) shared his company's customer service philosophy. He called it "Moments of Truth."

From the moment a passenger decides to fly SAS until he reaches his destination, he comes in contact with five SAS employees. Each employee must "win" when it's his turn with the customer.

"What good does it do if four employees 'wow' the customer and the fifth employee alienates him?" Carlzon asked. "The customer will remember the employee who

was rude or discourteous, thus making the whole flight a miserable experience."

This "destination point" approach to helping children is the same. A child has to win at each destination point. All of us—parents, family, teachers, coaches, club leaders, religious leaders, and even everyday citizens—have a responsibility to make sure kids have opportunities to be successful. We need to consciously ask ourselves, "What am I doing to make a difference in a child's life?"

I see how important it is to make sure that each contact a child experiences at school is a successful contact. If a student has contact with a bus driver, cafeteria helper, janitor, principal, vice-principal, nurse, and six teachers, there are a lot of opportunities for failed "Moments of Truth."

Mrs. Ramirez suggests the task is not the job. It doesn't come from a job description; it comes from the heart. The real job is to give children experiences that will help them be successful.

Treasure Hunter's Pledge

As an adult and a treasure hunter,
I am committed to search for all the talents, skills, and intelligence that exist in all children and youth.
I believe all children are capable of success,
No Exceptions!

Three

What Makes a Difference?

ROBERT and Mrs. Ramirez retreated to the faculty lounge for a refreshment.

"You seem a little tired, Mr. Dawson," observed the principal.

"I guess I am, but in a good way," Robert responded. "Here are my questions."

Robert questioned Mrs. Ramirez for the next 45 minutes about her school's history, its dramatic turnaround, and its exemplary programs. Mrs. Ramirez was patient in her responses and took her time to fully answer each question. But Mrs. Ramirez did not talk much about programs. She talked about the culture.

"Whether we know it or not, all schools, organizations, and communities have a culture. That culture can work for you, or it can work against you," offered Mrs. Ramirez.

"When our school was failing, which meant our students were failing, it was rooted in our culture, and it wasn't just in our school, it was throughout our community."

"The expectation from our history was that our students don't do well. They are not achievers, so they are not expected to achieve. And without thinking about it, we met those expectations. It became a self-fulfilling prophecy. We were on automatic pilot, going through the motions and not understanding how our culture was controlling us," Mrs. Ramirez explained.

"No program, curriculum, computer, or policy on the face of the earth is going to change a culture that is aimed at failure. We needed to change our culture, and to do that, we needed to understand what each of us truly believed in," she said.

"Believed in?" asked Robert. "What does that have to do with teaching our children?"

Robert had already forgotten about the *World's Most Important Question*.

"Everything," answered Mrs. Ramirez.

"You see, we didn't know what we believed in. We knew our mission was to teach our children. But did we, as individuals, truly believe that was possible? Many believed that if we just found the right program or the right curriculum, children would succeed. We were looking for the magic potion. There was no easy answer, but there was a *simple* answer. We did some serious soul searching. We asked every one of our staff—and that means everyone— to write out a personal mission statement as it related to children. We did that because most times we don't think of ourselves having a personal mission. That is something organizations craft. But we all do have missions; we just haven't ever spent the time to think it through."

As part of the school's professional development experiences, each faculty and staff person is asked to consider their role in the lives of children. If they were an organization of one, what would their personal mission statement read like as it relates to children?

Each person was challenged to express the benefits children experience through them. Some of the staff noted that they offered a listening ear; others suggested that their children felt cared for and wanted; some related that children felt their love, while others said they helped children set goals. The missions covered many examples associated with what the district's study learned about the types of relationships different adults offer to children. The realization from this activity was each adult has different strengths that they can offer children. Accordingly, it was acknowledged children need different relationships from adults at different times. Recognizing publicly what each adult believes are his or her strengths creates an inventory of missions that can be drawn from when needed. When a child needs comforting, who best can offer that relationship? When a child needs those special adults prepared to go the extra mile, where can they be found?

The second part of the exercise was designed to demonstrate how a mission connects to a belief system to create a culture.

"To truly create a culture, we needed our faculty and staff to personally connect to this effort," explained Mrs. Ramirez. "We shared the following statement that would frame the importance of relating to our newly defined culture:

Vision

A compelling idea, shared in the hearts of many, that moves people to exert personal energy, form vital alliances, and suspend self-interest to achieve the desired future... "a common good."

"The school defined *a compelling idea* as the paradigm shift from youth *at risk* to *Kids at Hope.*

"*Shared in the hearts of many*—We realized people would not accept the paradigm shift unless they could emotionally accept its importance. No amount of statistics or research would or could convince someone, who, for whatever reasons, could not accept the shift.

"*Moves people to exert personal energy*—reminded everyone the acceptance of the paradigm shift from *at risk* to *at hope* and the alignment of the culture required some level of action from every single person.

"*Form vital alliances*—suggested this could not happen in one part of the school or just with some people but not others. It also suggested we needed to look inside and outside of our schools for synergy.

"*Suspending self-interest*—was the key phrase needed to create a culture. Whether we want to think about it or not, the fact remains that all organizations and people act in accordance with their self-interest. The paradox is that you cannot create a culture if we retreat to our self-interests. The most common questions asked when a new effort is introduced are, what does this mean to me or what does it mean to the function of our school? The reality remains . . . we very rarely get to the critical question: What does it mean to our children? At this stage, participants are reminded that we weren't asking anyone to forfeit or abdicate self-interest but to *suspend it* in order to achieve together what we can't alone—supporting the success of all children, without exception.

"*A common good*—the school's common good was its belief that *all children are capable of success, No Exceptions*. But again, this could not be accomplished if we as individuals and the school as a whole could not accept this cultural belief."

"How did you get everyone on board with this understanding?" asked Robert.

"Simply, but powerfully," offered Mrs. Ramirez. "Remember we started this discussion by asking each person to consider and write out their personal mission statements. When you think about it, our personal mission statements represent to a very large degree our self interest. At this stage we reminded everyone that we weren't asking them go 'give up' their missions only to suspend them by allowing our cultural belief statement to be part of each individual's personal statement.

"This was accomplished by requesting that every person include at the end of his/her personal mission statement the word 'because,' and then finish their missions with the phrase: all children are capable of success, No Exceptions!"

What the school achieved through this process was the recognition that mission statements are owned, but belief systems are shared. To create a culture, there needs to be a thread that ties all the individual interests, i.e., missions, together, and that happens through the adoption of a belief statement that again is shared, not owned.

Through this exercise, some soul searching was taking place. The important question was now in front of everyone, and that was: are you able to suspend your self-interest and connect what you do individually to what needs to be achieved as a culture? The school wanted to know if the people responsible for teaching children truly believed that our children would succeed and understood how we can reach all youth without exception. Simply speaking, if they did not, then they did not belong on campus.

"It wasn't that they were bad people, it was that their personal mission statements were not compatible with our cultural belief system. We wouldn't allow the power of our belief to end up as empty words on a plaque in our halls," she said.

"Am I making sense, Mr. Dawson?" asked Mrs. Ramirez.

"Please continue," Robert replied.

"It is hard at first not to reduce our success to the mechanics of a program. It's imperative that this success begins with a belief system. Our culture is no more than acting out our beliefs," explained Mrs. Ramirez. "It is the sum total of our actions."

She went on, describing how the school drew its breath, its magic, and its life from each person on the campus.

"Again, I hate to say it, but many of our staff didn't believe all our children could succeed as we discovered when we asked them to complete the *World's Most Important Question*. When we collected all the survey responses, the average number scored between one and 10 was 6.5. When we randomly sampled our respondents in order to learn what prevented them from selecting number 10, the most offered answer had to do with the word *reality*. What we discovered was many people found it difficult to choose number 10 because they have too much information about children who struggle and fail. They read about children failing in the paper, see it on television and many times experience it personally."

"But isn't that just being honest?" questioned Robert.

"Yes, if you are focused just on the past and the present, but we are focused on the future," offered Mrs. Ramirez. "You see, we can't do anything about the past and very little about the present, but you can do a whole lot about the future. But only if you believe you can. If you can't believe you can affect the future, then you start giving up on kids, and that isn't acceptable. Again, the research is clear, students succeed when they are surrounded by adults who believe they can succeed. Our job is to ensure we are surrounding our children with adults who can circle or choose number 10.

"I hate to admit it, but we also had lots of students who bought into the belief that they were at risk."

"I see," Robert responded.

"Did you have good teachers, Mr. Dawson?" Mrs. Ramirez asked.

"Yes, I did," he replied.

"Did you have bad teachers?" Mrs. Ramirez continued.

"Yes."

"What was the difference," asked Mrs. Ramirez, "between the good teachers and the bad?"

"Well, let's see," answered Robert. "The good teachers seemed to believe in me." Robert offered the word believe without even thinking about it.

"Did you say 'believe?'" asked Mrs. Ramirez.

"In fact I did, but until you mentioned it, I didn't think about it. I didn't even realize how powerful that word is," noted Mr. Dawson.

Dawson continued, "They never gave up on me. They were always there for me. They had positive energy and high expectations of me."

"And the bad teachers?" Mrs. Ramirez asked.

"They seemed to go through the mechanics of teaching, but couldn't relate to the students," Robert said.

"That's right, Mr. Dawson!" she responded."When we think about our own experiences and how people helped us succeed, we remember the adults who believed in us.The students remember the teachers who believed in them, who supported them, who helped them succeed, not just in a subject matter, but in life," Mrs. Ramirez said.

"Your point, Mrs. Ramirez?" Robert asked.

"The point, Mr. Dawson, is that to *teach* a child, you must first *reach* a child!" exclaimed Mrs. Ramirez.

The point is, to teach a child, you must first reach a child.

Dawson's Reflection:

Have we forgotten those experiments in education from so long ago, The Pygmalion experiments I think they were called. The name was taken from the George Bernard Shaw Play "Pygmalion," later turned into a movie called

My Fair Lady. *In the musical, Eliza Dolittle said the only difference between a lady and a flower girl from the docks is the way you treat them. If you treat me like a flower girl from the docks, I'll behave like that. If you treat me like a lady, I'll behave like a lady. In the movie, she was accepted as the princess of the ball because she was treated that way. In the education experiments, if you thought a student was an underachiever, you tended to treat them that way. My freshman year of high school, they had four home rooms, 9A, 9B, 9C and 9D. 9A and 9B were the college prep classes and C and D were the lesser classes. Boy, talk about a subliminal message. Of course, every child may not win, but that's not the point, the adults in their lives must act as if they could. Years ago, I talked to a boy in juvenile detention and asked him what his parents would say about him ending up here. His answer still haunts me. "They'd be very proud." How often do adults unconsciously or unwittingly use labels to define children knowing full well that negative labels have never helped a child, never!*

Four

No Exceptions!

"OOPS, it's almost 11 o'clock. Time flies when you're having fun, right, Mr. Dawson?" asked Mrs. Ramirez.

"Right, Mrs. Ramirez," Robert responded.

"We have a meeting with our *No Exceptions Team* leader," Mrs. Ramirez said.

"No Exceptions Team?" Robert asked.

"Come along. I think you will find this meeting interesting," suggested Mrs. Ramirez.

"From what I have seen so far, I have no doubt about that fact," Robert replied.

Mrs. Ramirez and Mr. Dawson strolled over to Jim Smith's classroom. This was Mr. Smith's lunch period, and he scheduled a meeting with the principal to discuss his team's efforts.

"I took the liberty of having the cafeteria make up a few sandwiches," Mr. Smith said as his guests arrived.

"Thank you, Jim. This is Mr. Dawson," introduced Mrs. Ramirez.

"Yes, we knew you would be visiting today. So far, so good?" asked Mr. Smith.

"To say the least," Robert replied.

"Mrs. Ramirez asked if I would take a few moments and talk about our No Exceptions Team," Mr. Smith said.

"Please, I am anxious to hear about your program," encouraged Robert.

"Sorry, Mr. Dawson, this isn't a program. It's part of our culture," responded Mr. Smith.

"I apologize. I should know that by now. Old habits are tough to break," a contrite Robert noted. "I came here to learn about your exemplary programs, and I have yet to see one. I think I'm beginning to understand the culture concept, but I have to admit it does take awhile to internalize."

"Don't worry. We all were a little confused when we started," confessed Mr. Smith. "I was probably the worst of the naysayers on our faculty. When I heard that we were going to change our culture, I said, 'Here we go again, the new flavor-of-the-month syndrome.' I was wondering, how long will this flavor last? I was also concerned about the time and effort that would be required. You know teachers ... we are not short on things to do. Anything extra creates the impression that this could be the straw that breaks the camel's back."

"So what did you do?" asked Robert.

"Not much at first," offered Mr. Smith. "I approached this concept with the attitude that I would go through the motions, but my heart wouldn't be in it."

"What changed your mind?" Robert asked.

"Mrs. Ramirez scheduled an in-service training which I wasn't too keen about. But then everything began to change. It wasn't the typical in-service training of just more stuff," related Mr. Smith "And it wasn't just for the usual suspects."

"Please continue," Robert said.

"The training was focused on each and every one of us. The school invited all personnel, including our bus drivers, crossing guards, food service, and custodial staff. If it takes a village, we must include the village. It challenged us to look at ourselves, our successes. It challenged us to define success. It challenged us to recognize whether we were first, honest to ourselves, and what that means to our children. We explored not only our conscious attitudes about students but our unconscious attitudes as well. And it wasn't preachy. As a matter of fact, it was fun to recall the many people who helped us to succeed. We learned a concept called Success Links," continued Mr. Smith. "What we learned during the workshop was that there are a common set of experiences or links that have the power to help children succeed. And those links are within each of us and yet, over the years we tend to forget what they are."

"Well, what are they?" asked Robert.

"Too easy just to tell you. If I did, it would just be information. So let me just ask you about your own success," Mr. Smith offered.

"Sounds good; what do you want to know?" Robert asked.

Mr. Smith said, "I want you to think of a giant anchor chain in the form of an 'S.' This stretch of chain would require about 50 links."

"For an anchor chain to do its job, it must be strong. Now, think of each of those links as a Success Link, that is, a positive experience or person in your life that, in effect, strengthened your chain of development," Mr. Smith added.

"I just want you to think about those outside events or people who encouraged and supported you. In other words, what influenced your success?" Mr. Smith asked.

"You mean, like good teachers?" asked Robert.

"Yes, like good teachers, but also everything or everyone else you can think of that helped you to achieve your success thus far," suggested Mr. Smith.

"Well, I would have to say my parents were my first success, my first link," Robert stated.

"Think of a six-foot-wide sign inside that first link on a football field with your parents' names on it," interrupted Mr. Smith. "Other thoughts?" Mr. Smith continued.

"Teachers, some coaches, a close friend of the family and boy, I haven't thought about this person in a hundred years, but a man named Joe," Robert recalled.

"What did Joe do for you?" asked Mr. Smith.

"He smiled at me every day as I walked to school. He called me 'the brain' and made me laugh," answered Robert.

"Who was he?" asked Mr. Smith.

"The crossing guard," Robert replied with a smile.

"Anyone else or anything else that supported your success?" continued Mr. Smith.

"Let's see, my seventh-grade math teacher always believed I could master problems that seemed too difficult," recalled Robert. "I was never a good math student, but my math teacher believed in me—not just about math—but he seemed to just believe in me. He told me I could do anything I put my mind to. That's about it. Wait, I seem to recall that I learned that I was good at many things. I was good at sports, I was good in school, and I had a lot of friends. I think being good at things in your childhood helps you to succeed in adulthood," Robert said.

Mr. Smith interrupted, "Don't forget your Success Links. All those people and things you named must be reflected in a link."

Robert was reflecting on his answers. He was enjoying his brief journey back to those early years.

"Well, that's it!" interrupted Mr. Smith.

"That's what?" asked Robert.

"That's it!" exclaimed Mr. Smith. "I'm not trying to be cute or smart, but what you described is 'it.' You see, what you remember about growing up is true for most people who today believe in themselves and have experienced success. Simply put, we learned from our own experiences and the experiences of others, that if you offer children a set of Success Links, you can dramtically improve their chances to succeed. And how do we know? Because it worked for us and people like us. We also have the research to back that up as well.

"We understand that all people need food, water, and oxygen. We understand that all people need shelter and a sense of security. We need to also understand that all people, especially children, need a set of Success Links and experiences which improve their opportunities for success," Mr. Smith said.

"And what might those links be?" inquired Robert.

"Just what you said," responded Mr. Smith. "To help ensure a child's success. Our district's research findings helped us understand how these relationships are characterized by the behavior of the people in our lives. We learned about the associated behaviors of a good teacher, mentor, role model, and parent. It became very clear to us that we had to understand how children respond to the different adults in their lives. Some adults are able to reach children and others aren't. Some adults are toxic to children and others help children thrive."

Litany of the Links
The Success Links Chain of Robert Dawson

- My parents: for always having faith in me and for being there for me,
- Joe: our crossing guard who called me 'Einstein,'
- My seventh grade teacher: who always believed I could master problems that seemed too difficult,
- Sister Dominic: who befriended my family and always encouraged me,
- John: my best friend in grade school, for accepting me,
- Brother Roger: my high school counselor for four years,
- Brother Bob: who saw me through 60 hours of detention and kept me in the game,

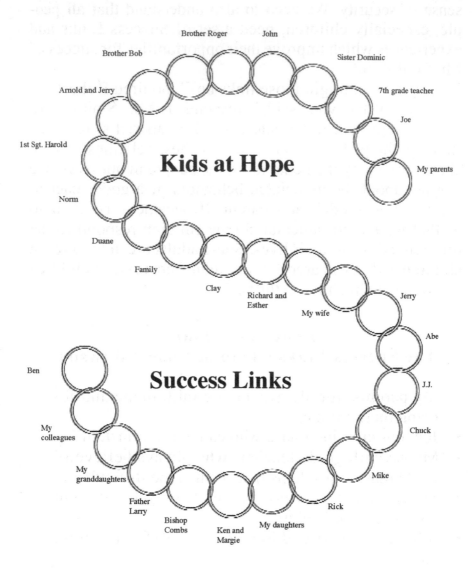

Brother Roger
John
Brother Bob
Sister Dominic
Arnold and Jerry
7th grade teacher
Joe
1st Sgt. Harold

Kids at Hope

My parents
Norm
Duane
Family
Clay
Richard and Esther
My wife
Jerry
Abe
Ben

Success Links

J.J.
My colleagues
Chuck
My granddaughters
Mike
Father Larry
Rick
Bishop Combs
Ken and Margie
My daughters

- Arnold & Jerry: my friends and employers,
- John: my best friend for a number of years, who taught me loyalty,
- 1st Sgt. Harold: he taught me the real skills of leadership,
- Norm: who taught me dedication and commitment,
- Diana: a co-worker and girlfriend, who taught me compassion,
- My brothers and my sisters-in-law: who taught me about FAMILY,
- Brother John: who taught me that everyone has something to offer the world,
- Clay: who taught me tenacity and allowed me to volunteer at his youth organization,
- Richard and Esther: life-long best friends, who taught me loyalty and compassion,
- My wife: who continues to teach me unconditional love,
- Jerry: my first boss who taught me the importance of training people,
- Abe: a friend and board member of my Boys' Club, who taught me about volunteerism and dedication,
- J.J. and John: my board presidents, who taught me what true volunteers are,
- Chuck: who hired me to run his camp and taught me acceptance,
- Mike: who taught me so much about philosophy and creativity,
- Rick: who hired and promoted me and who taught me to see beyond!
- My daughters: who taught and continue to teach me Joy,
- Ken and Margie: who continue to teach me friendship, acceptance and Spirit,

- Bishop Gomes: who reminded me of the importance of Faith and friendship,
- Father Larry: my pastor, who continues to teach me the power of values,
- My granddaughters: who have re-taught me the meaning of unconditional love,
- My colleagues: for sharing and unconditional acceptance . . . always!
- Ben: who has always supported me,
- Lynne: who loves me no matter what.

The Harrison School District was interested about the number of adults who influence a child each day. They created a simple process called "Kid Mapping," wherein a group of randomly selected students were followed for a of 24-hour period to determine the number of adults who would have an affect on them. In some instances, over 50 different adults were found to influence a single child from the moment he woke up until he went to bed.

These adults included parents, neighbors, school bus driver, crossing guard, campus security, food service personnel, custodians, teachers, administrators, after school activity directors, store keepers; the list was larger than first expected. Most importantly, though, was the recognition that children are exposed to a great number of adults every day. Every adult will either offer a child an emotional deposit or withdrawal.

The magnitude of this realization illuminated the notion about why some children do better in navigating life's challenges and opportunities while others do not. If children are exposed to adults who are unable to offer emotional support, or even worse are toxic to children, then the student's odds of success are diminished.

Furthermore, distinguishing the level of influence the schools control related to this understanding against what happens outside their control was needed.

The study concluded that the most powerful influences in a child's life have more to do with relationships than economics, social isssues, or home and family. Conditions such as poverty, single-parent homes, being born to an unwed teenage mother, gangs, drugs, and even abuse and neglect were trumped by the love, caring, inspiration, and the opportunity for children to succeed on their terms, not just others' expectations

The district identified those powerful relationships children require from adults as the four Aces. The metaphor was simple: Some children are dealt good cards in life, while others are dealt a lousy hand. In this metaphor, the best cards one can be dealt are:

When these findings were shared with the schools, the question was obvious. If children need Aces, and some students receive them and others don't, who controls the Aces? The answer was equally obvious. Adults do! The fact that some children receive Aces while others don't is the result of adults who consciously chose to make sure children receive Aces. One critical, fascinating, and empowering aspect of this part of the district's study was the demonstration that many children are able to do well inlife with just one Ace, and many times it wasn't the parent/ Ace of hearts. Equally dramatic was the understanding that in the absence of any Aces, a child is indeed doomed to struggle. But what cards you are dealt doesn't need to be left to chance. Understanding that was how the district empowered itself.

Mr. Smith noted that many adults have used the excuse that they are unable to help many students achieve due to the poor influences of others in the child's life. These adults have bought into the *at-risk* factors that they accept as a child's destiny rather than empower themselves with the knowledge that the greater influence in a child's life is dependent on the caring adults who choose to support a child's potential regardless of other influences.

Additional conclusions noted in the district's study:

•Children need Aces. Adults control the Aces. Any adult can considerably encourage and help shape a child's future.

•The more Aces a child receives, the greater the chance he/she can successfully navigate life's challenges and opportunities.

•Giving Aces has nothing to do with a job or social status. It has everything to do with what's written in your heart.

•When one adult cannot give an Ace to a child, it doesn't mean someone else can't. The important recognition is that all children need Aces, and if you can't seem to give an Ace to a student, find someone who can.

Those aces are represented by:

• **An anchor/parent:** someone responsible for a child's emotional and physical well being 24 hours a day, seven days a week, in an unconditionally loving way.

• **Other caring adults:** "The more the merrier," the more adults a child can perceive as caring about him/her, the greater his/her chance for success.

•**High expectations:** represented by someone who believes in you more than you believe in yourself, who believes you can achieve things you may not believe you are capable of achieving. These are our Treasure Hunters.

•**Opportunities to succeed:** Create a pattern of success. Acknowledge that failure breeds failure.

"So what does that have to do with your No Exceptions Team?" interjected Robert.

"My team's job," stated Mr. Smith, "is to work with the entire school and reach out to our community to ensure that our children leave our school with Aces in their hands, no exceptions!"

"I get it," shared Mr. Dawson. "The Success Links and the Aces represent Universal Truth number two; children succeed when they have meaningful and sustainable relationships with caring adults."

"BINGO!" shouted Mr. Smith.

Mr. Smith was pretty excited that Robert Dawson "connected the dots." The school understood that its research findings needed to go beyond general knowledge. It needed to be internalized by the faculty and staff. Unless adults could remember their own feelings of connectedness, abandonment, or isolation as children, they would be unable to connect in a meaningful and sustainable way with students.

The Aces metaphor also helped teachers, administrators, and support personnel to realize that connecting to children happens many different ways. Each Ace describes a different kind of relationship children need from adults. It also reminds us that it's impossible for one adult to give all four Aces to every child. Yet, every child needs one or more Aces to succeed.

Understanding Universal Truth number two and its implications for both adult and child unlocks the institution's capacity to ensure that every child is connected to a caring adult. Those adults can be the teacher, secretary, custodial staff, or food service personnel, not just the assistant principal, psychologist, counselor, or social worker. Again, it's the ability to differentiate an organizational structure or hierarchy from that of a culture. In an organization's structure, there is a clear line of command. Everyone has a job title and job description. It's all about operating the infrastructure. It has little to do with the mission that lies in the culture of the organization not in policies and procedures.

President John Kennedy, in his 1960 inaugural address, encouraged all citizens to "Ask not what our country can do for you, but what you can do for our country." President Kennedy was talking about America's culture, not its government. Culture and organizational hierarchies can coincide nicely. Those that have achieved that relationship are moving toward "greatness." Those that don't are stuck in being at best, "good."

"But how do you ensure that children are in fact receiving Aces? It sounds good in theory, but to be candid, it seems more wishful thinking than practical," offered a skeptical Robert Dawson.

"It does, doesn't it? That's what I thought, too," replied Mr. Smith. "When I first heard about the importance of Aces, I could not fathom how we could guarantee that all our children receive Aces until Mrs. Ramirez introduced 'Aces Tracking.'"

"Aces Tracking?" repeated Mr. Dawson.

"Yes, Aces Tracking," continued Mr. Smith. "You see, unless we have an objective measurement that all our children are receiving Aces, we are fooling ourselves and once again failing our children. Our goal was to take our good intentions and make them intentional."

"So, how does it work?" pursued Robert Dawson.

"We started tracking our Aces. We have a computer program where we can upload all our students' names as well as our Treasure Hunter's names. Each staff person is given a password that allows him or her to log onto the system, review each student's name, and depending on the type of relationship offered by the Treasure Hunter, they would record the associated Ace that best defines their relationship. If we see a student with limited Aces or no Aces, we know that student is disconnected. It raises a red flag and now we can do something about it."

Mr. Smith went on to describe that Aces Tracking is used after the first eight weeks from the start of school, and again after 24 weeks. After each Aces Tracking period, interventions are discussed for those students who are disconnected.

As importantly, when a student needs counseling or is experiencing social or emotional issues, those adults who are recorded Aces for the student may be called to assist with the intervention.

"We use the whole village," proudly stated Mrs. Ramirez.

Robert Dawson was pleased to learn how the school was monitoring, validating, and documenting the importance of relationships underscoring the school's commitment to its belief that all students can succeed, no exceptions, as well as it own research, which revealed the Three Universal Truths.

Harrison Schools Aces Tracking System

ACES TRACKING
Welcome to the Harrison School District's "Kids at Hope Aces Tracking System"! For the first time, schools will be able to track those meaningful and sustainable

relationships we know, and our research confirms, are critical to the success of all children, No Exceptions! After logging in to Aces Tracking system, your administrator will be able to download your school roster. Your faculty and staff (we call them Treasure Hunters) will then be able to log in and enter the appropriate symbolic "Ace" defining the level of the relationship/connection they have with a child. (Please see the "Aces Criteria" to define how one decides which Ace to designate.) This is a simple, but enormously powerful data collection and analysis program. After the data has been entered, the principal, director, manager, superintendent, or other authorized personnel, will have access to a report indicating which children are connected to caring adults and which are not. **This data system takes our good intentions to another level by ensuring that we are indeed intentional about our efforts to connect kids with caring adults.**

Again, this level of data is enormously consequential to the development of a culture that can demonstrate how all children succeed, No Exceptions!

If we truly believe and understand that it is the type of relationship that makes a difference, then this innovative and powerful program will support your valued efforts to connect children with caring adults.

Dawson's Reflection:

I traveled here to view a once-struggling school that is now singled out for its success. I heard about this school's innovative programs. I came to see those programs firsthand. After four hours, I have yet to see anything close to what I expected. But something is happening here; something special. The school's turnaround seems to be based not so much on a mission statement as a belief system that is internalized by its staff. Their belief that all children are capable of success

Aces Tracking System

A   **Ace of Hearts**

♥   **Anchor/Parent**

Responsible for a child's physical and emotional well being 24 hours a day, 7 days a week, 365 days a year in an unconditional, loving way.

Give this Ace to your own children—remind them how important they are.

A

♥

A   **Ace of Clubs**

♣   **Other Caring Adults**

All three criteria must be met to check this box:

1. You have known the child/ youth for at least eight weeks.
2. You can describe at least three very positive characteristics, skills, or talents you believe the child possesses.
3. You believe this child feels comfortable asking for your assistance.

A

♣

A   **Ace of Spades**

♠   **High Expectations**

All four criteria must be met to check this box:
1. You have known the child/youth for at least eight weeks.
2. You feel you believe in this child/ youth sometimes more than he/she believes in him/herself.
3. You sense that you are one of the "go-to adults" this child may contact if he/she wishes to discuss a problem/issue beyond an academic subject.
4. You have a sense for this child's/ youth's experiences during the non-school hours (i.e., a sense of home life/community life.) **A**

♠

A   **Ace of Diamonds**

♦   **Opportunities to Succeed**

All three criteria must be met to check this box:
1. You have given this child opportunities to succeed and have acknowledged his/her success.
2. When this child is with you, he/ she feels a sense of achievement and is valued and appreciated.
3. This child succeeds in your classroom/program/organization.

♦

does not stop there. It is then translated into a cultural framework that is then supported by a set of expressions.

My concern is that a culture is not as easily "canned" for public consumption as is a curriculum. We can put together manual materials; video and other support materials, mail them out and have schools adopt the elements. But how do you "can" a culture? How do you package a successful culture and replicate it? Seems like that may ultimately be the $64,000 question for Mrs. Ramirez and her staff.

Five

Defining Hope
Universal Truth III

MR. DAWSON, we are holding a call for you in the office," announced the school secretary over the intercom.

"Go ahead and use my office," offered Mrs. Ramirez. "I'll join you in a second."

"Hello, Dawson here!"

"Hi, Robert, this is Deborah. Sorry to disturb you, but I wanted you to know that the Secretary has called a big meeting for early Friday, and it's important that you be there."

"I'll be there," Robert replied, "Anything I should know about before the meeting?"

"We sent you a detailed email and some briefing papers," answered Deborah.

"I'll check it out. Thanks for the call," responded Robert.

"Is everything OK?" asked Mrs. Ramirez.

"Oh, yes. The Secretary of Education has called an important meeting for Friday, and all hands must be on deck," Robert explained.

"Are you ready to continue our tour, Mr. Dawson?" Mrs. Ramirez inquired.

"In a moment. But I do have one question. Something's bothering me," Robert replied.

"What is it?" Mrs. Ramirez asked.

"As you know, I came here to learn to about your program, but I have come to understand the remarkable culture and the belief system that you have created," he replied. "I am concerned that, although laudable and obviously effective, it may be difficult to replicate. What are your feelings?"

"Too early to answer that, Mr. Dawson. There is still one more Universal Truth we need to reveal before I am able to answer that question," Mrs. Ramirez replied.

"All right, I'm putting my trust in your good hands," Robert said.

Mrs. Ramirez went on to remind Mr. Dawson about Universal Truth numbers one and two. It was important for her to review these truths, as they are critical to the framework that encompasses the school's culture. Universal Truth Number One recognizes that *children succeed when they are surrounded by adults who believed they could succeed.* The second Universal Truth underscores the types of *meaningful and sustainable relationships students need from adults.*

Mrs. Ramirez then identified Universal Truth Number Three, which states that *children succeed when they can articulate their future at four destinations.* Mrs. Ramirez continued, "When children can articulate their future, we have helped to transform them from *at risk* to *at hope.*"

> **Universal Truth #3:**
> *Children succeed when they can articulate their future at four destinations.*

During the district's research, it examined studies about children and youth who were committed to juvenile detention or correction facilities. One of the recurring themes identified through interviews with incarcerated youth was their difficulty anticipating a future for themselves. The researchers defined that deficit as *Terminal Thinking*—the inability to see a future. Another descriptor would be *hopelessness*. In related research, the district learned about a concept known as *Mental Time Travel*, the ability to see one's future and feel empowered to achieve it. This powerful capacity is better known as HOPE.

The district immediately understood the consequences about both of these phenomena. It discussed the importance of "vaccinating" its students against *Terminal Thinking*, which leads to hopelessness. To achieve such a goal, the district understood the need to help students learn to *mentally time travel*. If this is achieved, students will develop the facility of HOPE. Robert was about to discover how Mrs. Ramirez's school vaccinated its students against hopelessness.

"I don't get it," responded Mr. Dawson.

"Come on, then. It's time for you to meet our Passport to the Future Advisory Committee," Mrs. Ramirez said.

"Passport where?" asked Robert.

"Come along," encouraged Mrs. Ramirez.

Mrs. Ramirez and Robert walked to the library. Waiting for them in a conference room were 12 people who had just gathered and were chatting informally.

As Mr. Dawson and Mrs. Ramirez entered, a man walked up to Robert and extended his hand.

"Hello, I'm Bill Modeleski, chairman of the Passport to the Future Advisory Committee."

"Robert Dawson, U.S. Department of Education."

"Good to have you here. Thanks, Mildred, for joining us. Time to get started."

"Our pleasure. Mr. Dawson and I will sit over here," Mrs. Ramirez said.

Mr. Modeleski asked everyone to be seated and formally welcomed Robert to the meeting.

The committee members then introduced themselves. The committee included two parents, Donald and Isabella Kelly; a pediatrician, Janet Osgood; the president of the neighborhood association, Michael Romero; a local community college instructor, Harold Byers; school police resource officer Don Pope; firefighter Dan Lewis; a representative from the city parks and recreation department, James Smith; chair of the No Exceptions Team, Carl Evans; school custodian Bob Anders; a representative of the local chamber of commerce, Karen Burns; and the executive director of a non-denominational faith-based ecumenical council, Paul Eppler.

"Looks like everyone made it today," observed Mr. Modeleski. "Mr. Evans, will you fill us in on the Passport to the Future Fair your committee has been planning?"

"Everything is on track," reported Mr. Evans. "We are planning on using the play field this year instead of the field house. We have a sub-committee chair for each of life's destination points: Home and Family, Education and Career, Community and Service, and Hobbies and Recreation. Our theme this year is 'The Successful Journey.'

"Each student will receive a 'Passport to the Future,' and each destination page will have at least five blanks for stamps that the students must earn to successfully pass through that destination point. The stamps will be placed on the passport according to the destination point that is being visited."

"Could you give us an example of how a student earns a stamp?" Mr. Modeleski asked.

"Sure," answered Mr. Evans. "We have invited fellow Treasure Hunters from all over the community. We divide them into each destination point. A group is assigned Home and Family, another Education and Career, and so on. The students then visit each destination point and 'interview' our guests. They try to determine what talents, skills, traits, characteristics, and intelligence each Treasure Hunter needed to succeed at their destination point. The goal is to identify as many different skills, talents, etc. needed to succeed at each of life's destination points.

"In other words, we are reinforcing the concept that success happens on the journey to life's destination points," continued Mr. Evans. "We wish to also reinforce that success in life requires many talents and skills, including reading, writing, math, and science in addition nonacademic areas, such as honesty, integrity, a sense of humor, and unselfishness. And finally, we recognize that life's journey will include a number of challenges and roadblocks.

"In fact," Mrs. Ramirez interjected, "at the end of the fair, group sessions called *Challenge Reviews* allow students and adults to discuss the challenges and opportunities they will discover on their journey. What we are achieving through this process is what our research calls *mental time travel*. We are deliberately training the brain to be hopeful. That is no different than training the brain to learn to read or write or solve a math problem."

Mrs. Ramirez signaled to Robert to join her outside the library's conference room.

"As you have witnessed, Mr. Dawson, our programs and activities are enhancements to our belief system and culture," Mrs. Ramirez said, "However, it seems that every year or so, a new initiative is passed by the school board, state legislature, or department of education," Mrs. Ramirez explained. "Each has a new or different idea as to what is supposed to happen within the four walls of our school.

Some people believe we are just about academics. Some think constant testing is the answer. Others believe we are here to teach values. Some groups advocate for character education. Others feel the school must also be a social service agency. We have many expectations placed on us, and each one seems to be disconnected from the other. Our priorities seem to constantly shift."

"So, what did you do about it?" asked Robert.

"We realized the success of our efforts in school along with those of the home and our larger community are dependent on each other," answered Mrs. Ramirez. "After stripping away all the politics, the self-serving interests, and the confusion, we concluded that although we have different jobs, we share the same responsibility as it relates to our children. That responsibility is to help our children prepare for their journey to the future. That future has to be defined. It extends beyond encouraging our youth to focus just on their careers. As adults, we know that life's journey is more than just getting a job. It's about helping children understand the four major destinations on life's journey; home and family; education and career; community and service; and hobbies and recreation. Together those four destinations define where the future lies," she said.

"That was a powerful conclusion, continued Mrs. Ramirez, "because it gave meaning to the word *future* not just to a set of skills and knowledge required to get a job but also by recognizing the talents, skills, and other intelligences that are required to succeed at each of life's four major destination points."

"That's amazing, Mrs. Ramirez," declared Robert.

"We think so, too," agreed Mrs. Ramirez.

"The fact that you identified life's four major destinations establishes a framework that makes all we do with children less fragmented and more holistic," Robert offered. "Furthermore, the four destinations are all-encompassing and engage a community to support the success factors needed in life. I am also intrigued by your efforts to communicate the understanding that life requires many talents for success. By doing so, students realize how many different opportunities there are to succeed.

"That's an important observation," noted Mrs. Ramirez. "When I was growing up in a little community, we were offered four sports in which to participate. If we wished to participate in athletics, our choices were football, basketball, baseball, and track and field. Oh, did I forget to note that those sports were only available to boys? So if you were a girl, you were on the sidelines as well as those boys who didn't relate to those four sports."

"I think I am getting your point, but please continue," Robert said.

"Well, if you only offer four sports and only for a select group of people, then you limit the number of opportunities for all children to succeed athletically," responded Mrs. Ramirez.

"Today, if you return to that community, you will see dozens of sports offered to both boys and girls and the end result is that you will see more boys and girls succeeding athletically," Mrs. Ramirez explained.

"Again, you are suggesting that we often limit the opportunity for our children to succeed," Robert asked.

"Not only am I suggesting it, I am saying it's still a fact of life and we are in the 21st century," replied Mrs. Ramirez. "In too many schools, we tell our students that success is limited to reading, writing, math, and science. I see this the same way I witnessed the four-sport limitation in my small community. As soon as we created more sports in which children could succeed, the more children we found succeeding. The reality is, that although reading, writing, math, and science are critical, there are other intelligences that are equal to those, and we should equally acknowledge and reinforce them as well. There is no upside to limiting the ways children can succeed."

Mrs. Ramirez also shared some insights she gleened during the Kids at Hope community trainings. "During one of our training activities, we ask the adult participants in the room to share their earliest thoughts about what they wanted to be when they grew up. Without exception, every participant listed a job, profession or occupation. They covered the gamut from doctor, lawyer, professional athlete, veterinarian, fire fighter, teacher, police officer, rock star, and so forth."

"What's so odd about that?" questioned Mr. Dawson.

"At first nothing, until it dawned on me . . . isn't it a bit strange that everyone replied to the open-ended question the same way?

"Huh?" was all that Mr. Dawson could offer, which was reinforced by the blank look in his eyes.

"Everyone answered with a job category. It was odd, because we had understood and accepted that success in life is about contributing to life's four major destinations: Home and Family, Education and Career, Community and Service, and Hobbies and Recreation. Yet, we have become so programmed during our upbringing to limit our thoughts about the future to just a job, profession, or occupation when we know our roles and contributions in life must extend well beyond a single dimension," continued Mrs. Ramirez.

Mrs. Ramirez was so taken by her observation that she asked her teachers if they would ask the same question of their students.

"What happened?" quizzed Robert.

Mrs. Ramirez noted that the answers were just as dramatic, but not surprising. The students limited their sense of future to just a job, profession, or occupation, similar to the adults.

"Our children need to understand that their futures are not limited to a job, even though that is important. But equally important is their understanding that the future includes family, community, and hobbies and recreation. Life is multidimensional," discussed Mrs. Ramirez.

"Absolutely," agreed Mr. Dawson, "As adults, we realize that life is more than just a job. The happiest of people are those who have found success and achievement in all aspects of their life, not just in one."

"You are correct, sir!" quipped Mrs. Ramirez. "So you can see we need to continue to explore and develop our children's talents and skills beyond just the ability to get a job but the capacity to contribute to the many opportunities that will be a part of their futures."

"Your insights underscore the importance of ensuring that we develop our young people's emotional and moral intelligences," shared Mr. Dawson.

"Absolutely, answered Mrs. Ramirez. "How important is it to society to have honest people? Or caring people? Or unselfish people?" she asked.

"Wow, it all sounds great," Robert responded.

"Hold on a second, Mr. Dawson. We have come a long way, but we don't pretend we have answered all the mysteries of the universe," Mrs. Ramirez replied with a mildly scolding tone.

"Oh, I know that, Mrs. Ramirez. But my excitement is focused more on what you have accomplished rather than what you haven't. You've created a simple, yet powerful framework, which not only rallies your school, but your entire community to be a part of that journey."

"Now you are getting it, Mr. Dawson," Mrs. Ramirez replied.

" I am, I am," Robert thought. "Success is what happens on the journey, and the more success opportunities you offer children, the more successful and hopeful children you will have."

Success is what happens on the journey, and the
more success opportunities you offer children, the more
successful children you will have.

Hope: The capacity to see one's future
(mental time travel) and feel empowered to achieve it.
Future=4 Destinations=HOPE

Dawson's Reflection:

I always believed that my goal was to "arrive" at my destination. In truth, the journey was as important as the destination, along with the realization that there was more than one destination where one needs to "arrive." The career position I have is more the result of my experiences than my promotions! All the ups and downs, all the wins and disappointments, all the pain and sorrow, prove I am the composite of my experiences.

More importantly, these experiences, including the skills, the talents, and the intelligence I have acquired, have real-world value. As I arrive at each destination point, including home and family, education and career, community and service, and hobbies and recreation, I'm better equipped to continue my success. But most importantly, without knowing it was those experiences, were also part of learning about Hope. And equally important, having that concept internalized. I began without realizing it to mentally time travel. Yet, my capacity to be hopeful and to mentally time travel to life's four major destinations did not happen by accident; it was deliberate, encompassing all of what Mrs. Ramirez refers to as the Three Universal Truths.

Six

Hope Square
(Hope²)

THE ALARM startled Robert. He hit the snooze button on his clock, hoping for a few more minutes of sleep.

It took Robert a couple of moments to fully awaken. He rubbed his eyes and stretched. "Time to tackle the world," he thought.

He glanced over at his schedule for the day. His first appointment was with Mrs. Ramirez and Dennis Tinseth. Mr. Tinseth was a high school principal. Mrs. Ramirez's young students would attend ultimately attend Mr. Tinseth's high school.

Mrs. Ramirez met Robert at his hotel at 7:30 a.m. Together, they had an 8 a.m. appointment with Mr. Tinseth.

"How far is the high school?" asked Robert.

"We aren't going to the high school. We are headed to the community youth center, which is just across the street from the high school," offered Mrs. Ramirez.

"Are we still meeting with Mr. Tinseth?" Robert inquired.

"Yes, but I want you to also meet Scott Trujillo, director of the community center," noted Mrs. Ramirez.

Robert was a bit perplexed by the schedule change but was anxious to learn as much as he could about the powerful culture he was discovering. He considered the visit with a high school principal a bonus. And he was also pleased that he would be visiting a youth center. Robert would be witnessing the Kids at Hope culture outside the four walls of an institution, as well as inside.

Robert and Mrs. Ramirez arrived at the community youth center. Scott Trujillo was outside admiring the center's new sign. Garfield Community Youth Center was in bold letters with a smaller, but still visible graphic appearing below: Kids at Hope Believed and Practiced Here.

"What do you think, Mrs. Ramirez?" asked Scott Trujillo.

"Pretty neat. Looks great," responded Mrs. Ramirez.

"Did you notice the new paint job?" Scott asked.

"I did," Mrs. Ramirez replied.

"This is Robert Dawson," Mrs. Ramirez said as she introduced the two men.

"Nice to meet you," a courteous Scott Trujillo acknowledged.

"Same here," Robert said.

A moment later, Mr. Tinseth arrived.

"Great sign, Scott," observed Mr. Tinseth.

"Thanks. Has your sign gone up yet?" Scott asked.

"Not yet. We are scheduled next week. They still need to put up the library and park signs," reported Mr. Tinseth.

"Hello, Dennis," interjected Mrs. Ramirez.

"Hi, Mildred," Mr. Tinseth answered.

"Meet Robert Dawson," added Mrs. Ramirez.

The men shook hands and exchanged pleasantries. "The more we export our cultural belief throughout our community, the greater chance we have to realize our belief," stated Mrs. Ramirez. "As I said earlier, we have to demonstrate those beliefs in everything we do. That is remarkably different from our old habits. Those old habits encouraged us to do our own thing, in our own way. Youth centers did their own thing, parks and libraries did their thing, the high school did its thing, and so on and so forth."

"That needed to change. Remember our discussion about self interest, asked Mrs. Ramirez.

"I do," answered Robert.

We need to continue to find ways to suspend that self-interest if we are to truly reach all our children . . . a greater common good. We sought creative ways to express our three universal truths in deeds," continued Mrs. Ramirez.

All the youth-serving organizations in the community took great pride in their individuality but unfortunately forgot that children don't grow up in one organization over another but are the sum total of all their experiences.

"We are all working with the same children, yet it wasn't that long ago that you wouldn't know that from the way we didn't work with each other," stated Scott Trujillo.

Scott Trujillo continued, "Therefore, we wanted to express our shared vision as visually as we could. In order to do this, we each agreed to give up a little of our individual identity for a greater good. What we decided to do is what you are now witnessing," Scott continued. "You see, we are all erecting new signs on our individual buildings to link our shared belief system."

"The fact we don't view children to be 'at risk,' but rather 'at hope,' is a unifying statement that does not require us to give up our unique missions. It not only allows us to strengthen our overall shared culture but also to better define it," Mrs. Ramirez said.

"The citizens of Harrison can drive by the high school, elementary school, community youth center, park, library, and other organizations and recognize that their youth serving organizations share a common belief. They are linked not only through signage, but through spirit and effectiveness to do whatever is necessary to ensure the success of all our children. Even our police cars bear a *Kids at Hope Community* sticker.

"The police are a highly visible presence in our community. They are easily recognizable. They offer many services to children and youth beyond law enforcement. They understand the importance of having children succeed. Recruiting the police department to join in this belief system and culture underscores the importance of our efforts," proudly stated Mrs. Ramirez.

"As our mayor recently said during a television interview when she unveiled the newly branded Kids at Hope police cars, 'Something important is happening in our city,'" Mrs. Ramirez said.

"So what you are saying, is that each organization or institution that buys into the shared belief system promotes that relationship?" Robert asked.

"Not only that, Mr. Dawson," continued Mrs. Ramirez, "businesses will also connect, because we are ultimately all here for the same reason, and that is to pass the torch of leadership and success from one generation to another. When an organization displays the *Kids at Hope Believed and Practiced Here* graphic they are announcing that their institution, department, or agency believes all children can succeed, No Exceptions; if you need an Ace, you can count on these groups to connect with children; and lastly here is a place where Hope is instilled by helping children articulate their future at four destinations,"

"Fascinating," Robert thought. "A whole community linked together."

"You see, Mr. Dawson, if we only showed you our school without the rest of the components, you'll only be able to explain how our culture works on campus. You may even mistakenly refer it as a program, rather than the shared culture that it is. The bigger picture may be lost. Kids don't grow up in institutions or agencies. They grow up in cultures. What we are trying to establish is a belief system and structure that supports the success of all our kids. To see all our children as 'at hope.' Remember your earlier question, 'Can this be replicated?'" asked Mrs. Ramirez. "The answer is, 'It depends!' It depends on whether or not the community can agree on the fact that all children are capable of success, *NO EXCEPTIONS!*"

"Looks like you are really thinking outside the box," Robert responded.

"That's an interesting observation," answered Mrs. Ramirez. "I used to think I was capable of thinking 'outside the box.' However, I wasn't good at thinking outside of my four walls," Mrs. Ramirez explained.

"There is quite a difference between thinking outside the box and outside your walls! That's a bigger challenge," she added.

"You mean not only do we need to think outside the box to help all children succeed, but we need to be able to think outside our four walls as well?" Robert asked.

"Exactly," answered Mrs. Ramirez. "Follow that up with thinking outside our city, county, and state boundaries, until our entire country can see all its children as 'at hope.' Unless we do, we will continue to fulfill our own *at-risk* prophecy.

Mrs. Ramirez reminded Robert Dawson that each year there are breakthroughs in medicine, engineering, space exploration and other sciences. But where are the breakthroughs in education? Unfortunately, communities are still locking up too many children, too many youth aren't finishing their basic education, too many are still joining gangs or taking drugs, and too many are still going through life aimlessly. It's time education and youth services find the necessary leadership and research to dramatically affect those trends. Mrs. Ramirez and her colleagues believe the three universal truths are part of that answer. The question then, is commitment.

"I also think I am beginning to better understand the difference between being a manager and a leader," offered Robert.

"You are?" asked Mrs. Ramirez.

"A manager thinks inside his or her organization, while a leader understands the importance of leading from the outside in," explained Mr. Dawson.

"Well said," answered Mrs. Ramirez. "I am trying to be a leader."

"I'm afraid to ask, but what's next?" inquired Robert.

"Funny you asked," answered Mr. Tinseth.

Mrs. Ramirez described her community's efforts in working with the city government to officially designate an area as Hope Square.

"I know it may sound a little silly, but we are very serious about that description symbolized by the word 'hope.'

"What's a Hope Square?" quizzed Robert.

"The idea came from our history. Do you remember learning about Town Squares?" inquired Mrs. Ramirez.

"You mean a place where the citizens of a town would gather to discuss the politics of the day, conduct commerce, or just socialize?" noted Robert.

"That's it. Our question was, 'What would such a place look like that allows a community to rally around its children?' Where we can connect. So our Hope Square suggests several things: First it is about promoting Hope community wide. Second, it's a location. We identify all the businesses, youth services, schools, and families that live in approximately a one-mile radius or the attendance area of an elementary school.

Third, *Square* has a separate meaning. Not only a location but when we succeed by having the community collaborate in such a powerful way, we have doubled the opportunity for all children to grow up hopeful. In other words, we Squared Hope (Hope^2) to the second power.

"By going to all this effort, we remind ourselves every day that we are interconnected and interdependent. We note the children we serve are not just one organization's children; they are all of our children," added Mr. Tinseth.

The group was soon joined by the library director and parks and recreation superintendent. The manager of a nearby fast-food restaurant also stopped by. In just moments, many important people who played a number of different roles in the success of children, were all outside the Garfield Community Youth Center admiring the new sign and graphics.

"Very impressive, very impressive," Robert repeated in private reflection.

"Any thoughts?" asked Mrs. Ramirez.

A community that cares about its children must express such caring in anything and everything it does.

Seven

High Fives

WHERE are we off to now?" asked Robert.

"It's a surprise," offered Mrs. Ramirez.

"I think you've done a pretty good job surprising me already," Robert joked.

"We are still missing a crucial element on this journey," offered Mrs. Ramirez.

"Aha! The high school! I was hoping we would get around to visiting the high school," Robert said.

"Right! The reason for doing what we do: and that is, to help every child succeed, no exceptions!" exclaimed Mrs. Ramirez. "This couldn't happen if our students didn't believe in what we are doing. Accordingly, it wouldn't work if the students weren't completely involved."

Mrs. Ramirez drove Robert over to the local high school.

As the two walked onto campus, a student greeted them.

"Hello, Mrs. Ramirez. My name is David. We are waiting for you by the student quad area."

David escorted his two guests to the picnic table where six other students waited.

Mrs. Ramirez asked the students to explain their roles in the belief system of success.

Sarah, a junior at the high school, began by explaining that she heard about a meeting where a belief system was to be explained and that students were being recruited to help. "I wasn't sure what they were looking for, but I was curious enough to attend," she said.

"What I learned was what I already felt deep inside. I learned, however, that it was important that such a belief must be shared with everybody, all the time," she added.

"And in your words, Sarah, what was that belief?" asked Robert.

"The belief was that every student is capable of success, no exceptions," answered Sarah.

"What could you do to support that statement, Sarah?" Robert asked.

"Let me answer that question," interrupted Daniel, a 17-year-old senior at the high school.

"Sure, go ahead," Sarah agreed.

Daniel added, "More than anyone, at this age, kids have a great influence over other kids. We can support our friends' dreams, encourage their hopes, or do the opposite. Too many kids think it's cool to step on other people's dreams. There are, however, a lot more of us who understand that to be a friend, you must support your friends' dreams. We understand that it takes a lot of support to succeed in life, and kids can help other kids succeed."

"How do you do that?" Robert inquired.

"My turn," offered Lynne a another junior at the school.

"Go for it," encouraged Daniel.

"Simple," suggested Lynne. "We share our dreams openly and honestly. We share our strengths. We also explore our weaknesses and what we can do to strengthen them. But our real focus is on our strengths. We work to remain optimistic, and we find the best way to do that is to have people around us who encourage us, care about us, and support us. In return, it is our responsibility to do the same for them and others."

"That's right," Candace, a 15-year-old sophomore offered. "High school is tough enough. The last thing we need is a campus that is a 'downer.' That's not to say we don't have our tough times. It just means that we make an earnest attempt at keeping the hope alive on campus. Each student, faculty member, administrator, cafeteria worker, school resource officer, everyone is part of the effort. We don't let anyone off the hook."

"How did you launch this effort?" Robert asked.

"About two years ago, when we were arriving on campus for the start of another school day, we were greeted at the front of the campus by all the teachers, principal, assistant principals, and staff," David said. "They were holding signs that stated that they believed in us. They were cheering us, throwing confetti at us, and handing out balloons. It seemed silly, but I have to confess, it lifted our spirits. We couldn't help but smile at the teachers and staff.

"That greeting was the beginning of our new culture on campus. Everyone began to pull together. Now that I look back on that day two years ago, I realize that something special was happening on our campus," David continued.

"Our school was prepared to do whatever was necessary to ensure the success of its students. I got excited about that. What we didn't realize, was that this was also the beginning of our entire community coming together around the same belief system," David said.

The discussion with the students continued with great spirit for another hour.

"Thank you, everybody," Robert responded. "You just put a giant explanation point on a truly remarkable two days. I wish you all well, and I can't wait to come back and spend more time with all of you."

Mrs. Ramirez drove Robert back to his hotel so he could get his rental car and head off to the airport. During their drive together, Mrs. Ramirez confessed getting the high school on board wasn't easy.

"For some reason, we begin to abandon our children during this most critical phase of their lives. We struggled with our middle school and high school administrators and staff to understand the Three Universal Truths. Children in middle and high school need to know adults believe in them, are there for them in meaningful ways, and are willing to help them understand and navigate life's four destinations. Even though the research is clear that children and youth of all ages need this type of culture to truly thrive, we have unfortunately ignored these finding in our middle and high schools."

As they approached Robert's hotel, Mrs. Ramirez took a few moments to underscore highlights of Mr. Dawson's two-day visit. She emphasized the Three Universal Truths that formed the framework of the school, district, and community's shared culture. In addition, she reminded Mr. Dawson that there were five accepted practices that have been designed to support and advance the culture. Those practices were witnessed by Mr. Dawson. They include:

1) Belief: the ability for everyone on campus to articulate a shared belief that *all children are capable of success, No Exceptions*;

2) Pledge: all students recite the Kids at Hope Pledge to reinforce the belief system and to personally internalize its message;

3) Report Card: the opportunity to focus on and celebrate a child's potential.

4) Passport to the Future: an experience and document which helps children understand their future; develop the capacity for Mental Time Travel thereby achieving hopefulness;

5) Aces Tracking: monitoring, documenting, and validating that all students are connected in a meaningful and sustainable manner with a caring adult.

Kids at Hope HIGH FIVE
Schools, Organizations, and Communities:
1)Belief
2)Pledge
3)Report Card
4)Passport to the Future
5)ACES Tracking

Robert thanked Mrs. Ramirez for two wonderful and exciting days.

Mrs. Ramirez thanked Robert and asked for one last favor. "Mr. Dawson, we need your leadership and desire to ensure that we remind our schools and all communities that we know how to help all children succeed. Knowing is one thing, desire to do something about it is something entirely different.

"You can count on me," responded Mr. Dawson.

Robert's final thought as the plane lifted off the ground was, if the future is all about our kids, then everything we do must relate to the future of our kids.

Dawson's Reflection:

Whoa, this goes way beyond "Moments of Truth" and boomerangs! This idea of total involvement is really what drives the culture of Kids at Hope. No one is exempt. We all have a role to play in our community in the development of our kids.

I remember speaking to a cast member at Disney World who told me that everyone is important to the success of the theme park because they all have a role in the show! Everyone's participation, encouragement, and support make Disney World a success. It's reflected in the memories people take away from visits there.

I remember a time when my grandmother, Jessie, was 83 years old and in the hospital. One night, waking up a bit disoriented, she got out of bed, grabbed her intravenous fluid stand, still wearing her nightgown, started down the hall toward the hospital's main entrance. It was 2 a.m. and a cold winter in Chicago.

Harold, a janitor working the graveyard shift, saw her leaving and acted quickly. He gently blocked her way, read her hospital identification tag and said, "Jessie, what in the world are you doing out here? It's cold outside. Let me get you back to your room."

I heard about the incident later that morning and asked the head nurse, "How did the janitor know to do this instead of just continuing to do his janitorial chores?"

Amazed by my question, she replied, "Mr. Dawson, everyone in this hospital takes part in providing health care service."

Indeed, everyone does have a role in the show and the same is true for a community. We must all be involved in raising our kids.

Eight

Mr. Dawson Goes to Washington

IT was 5:30 a.m. when Robert Dawson awoke in his Washington, D.C. townhouse. It was Friday and he had to be at the U.S. Department of Education headquarters by 7:30 a.m.

He completed his morning routine in half the time. He caught the metro subway into the district and arrived at his office a full half-hour before the meeting with the Secretary of Education was to begin.

He looked over his notes. He realized the secretary called this emergency meeting to discuss a policy crisis. Still, Robert asked the secretary's chief of staff to allow him 10 minutes in front of the secretary to discuss issues that he felt were enormously important. His request was approved. However, he was granted only five minutes to speak.

"Packed agenda," was the chief of staff's explanation.

It was almost 7:30 a.m. and Robert hurried down the hall to take his seat in the secretary's conference room.

Most of his colleagues had arrived early, and at exactly 7:30 a.m., the Secretary of Education arrived.

"Thank you all for joining me this morning," the secretary began." I understand some of you had to cut short your out-of-town trips and postpone meetings. I apologize for the inconvenience, but I felt it important to call the senior staff together to address a major policy issue which the president has asked us to review and formulate opinions on. The president plans to address these issues and our findings at his news conference Monday morning."

The secretary continued, "Four days ago, the President's Commission on the Future of America's Children released its report. The report raised a number of issues about our children and their futures. The report's three major findings included:

"1. America's children have great difficulty relating their educational experiences to real-world values. Too many students are not connecting what our schools are teaching to what they need to succeed as adults.

"2. America's children do not believe their futures to be bright.

"3. America's children believe that adults are detached from children's lives and therefore, children only get token support when support is needed.

"After the release of the study, every major news service and newspaper ran stories with these headlines," the secretary said.

- **"FUTURES BLEAK FOR YOUTH"**
- **"CHILDREN LACK HOPE"**
- **"WHERE HAVE ALL THE ADULTS GONE?"**
- **"HOPELESSNESS MAJOR CONCERN FOR AMERICA'S YOUTH"**

"So, ladies and gentlemen, our task is to offer the president some options, to address what he and I believe to be a crisis of 'hope.' In a personal call to me, the president noted he was very concerned," the secretary said.

"The president told me that 'America is the country that was built on hope. America's youth are its flame. America's youth are our future. If they don't see a bright future for themselves, then America doesn't have a bright future. It's as simple as that,'" he continued.

"I'm open to suggestions," concluded the secretary.

It was hard for Robert not to spring to his feet. He'd just spent so much time learning about hope. Now, he faced the Secretary of Education, who was asking for suggestions about what to do with a crisis concerning America's youth.

"Mr. Secretary," Robert spoke.

"Yes, Robert. Please, what insights to you have?" the secretary asked.

"Sir, I spent the past two days visiting a school that was identified as offering exemplary programs. I left my visit with a greater understanding that America's future and the solutions to its problems do not lie with another well-meaning program, but rather, are rooted in the same foundation that has existed since 1776. That foundation, Mr. Secretary, is our country's belief that all of its children can be successful, and there are no exceptions!" explained Robert excitedly.

"Mr. Secretary," Robert continued, "let me share with you a most remarkable experience, with the guarantee that the president and all Americans have little to be concerned with, if we can effectively challenge our nation to see its children more positively and encourage everyone to support our children's futures."

"Go on, Mr. Dawson," requested the secretary.

"Well, it starts with, 'You gotta believe!' Let me elaborate ..."

Conclusion

From Parable to Reality
The Kids at Hope Story Continues

DON'T be fooled into believing that our story is too naïve to possibly be true. The fact is, this story reflects the successes of the many groups, organizations, institutions, and agencies across the country that have adopted the Kids at Hope Three Universal Truths and High Five Practices. These courageous organizations have come to understand that it isn't a program that makes a difference in a child's life; it is first and foremost our belief in them, followed by meaningful relationships with caring adults and finally the understanding of the importance of focusing on their futures which is their accepting the gift of *HOPE*. Only then can the programs we provide ever make a difference.

Contact Kids at Hope at *www.kidsathope.org* to learn more about the communities and groups across the country that are modeling the examples offered in this book.

Kids at Hope provides professional staff and volunteer development, consulting, coaching, and program enhancements. Research and evaluation are available to support the goals and objectives associated with creating a culture where all children can succeed without exception.

Please contact us if you share our belief that our children are *at hope* rather than *at risk* and wish to learn more or to join the thousands of individuals and groups in this powerful initiative.

A Sampling of Case Studies from Across the Country

(The following six case studies were written by
Mary Ellen Collins)

The Pioneers of Hope
Phoenix

School district superintendent Ron Richards has achieved an important distinction for the 14 elementary and middle schools under his direction. His Pendergast School District was the first in the nation to adopt the Kids at Hope youth development strategy district-wide. All 10,000 students now have teachers, administrators, bus drivers, food service workers and playground aides who've embraced a belief system that states, "All children are capable of success, No Exceptions."

Richards initially offered one of his school principals the opportunity to attend the Kids at Hope training, but he vividly recalls the moment he realized it had to go beyond just one school.

"I had just heard that a teacher in one of my schools told a child that he would never amount to anything more than a custodian, and I thought, 'How could anyone burst a child's dreams that way?' That was the straw that broke the camel's back. I decided I wanted this to be a district where every single school adopts the Kids at Hope model. I wanted every single principal and teacher to be trained."

The research-based Kids at Hope model includes Universal Truths that state, "Children succeed when they are surrounded by adults who believe they can succeed, and when they have meaningful and sustainable relationships with caring adults."

Richards didn't expect 100% overnight change, but he stayed focused on his goal of eventual 100% buy-in. He says that the first year, a third of the schools exceeded expectations as far as implementing the model, a third met his expectations, and a third didn't quite meet expectations. In three years, the entire district has adopted the Kids at Hope model.

Pendergast students start their day with the pledge: *I am a Kid at Hope. I am talented, smart, and capable of success. I have dreams for the future and I will climb to reach those goals and dreams every day. All kids are capable of success, No Exceptions.*

Although some of Richards' teachers thought the middle schoolers would consider themselves "too cool" for things like the pledge, he counseled them to keep trying and to keep expecting it. And now, they say it as automatically as they say the Pledge of Allegiance.

"We underestimate the power that positive talk has for kids," says Richards, who goes on to recount some meaningful validation he received from the principal of University High, a school with a very competitive admissions process.

"When [the principal] asked one young applicant why she was pursuing the opportunity to attend University High, she replied, 'Because I have goals and dreams for the future.' When you start to hear your words come back to you, that's when you know you've touched someone."

Pendergast teachers also use other tools, like the Kids at Hope Report Cards—the only report card where kids cannot fail. The cards acknowledge *all* of a child's talents, successes, and their value to society and consequently instill hope and optimism about their future.

"People thought kids would be throwing them away, and every one of those report cards made it home," says Richards. "They're such positive rewards. The kids were really proud."

At a recent district strategic planning conference, teachers, staff, students, and community members talked about the culture and climate of the schools, what was working, and what they needed to do differently.

"The feedback from the kids was very, very powerful," says Richards. "They said that before Kids at Hope they didn't feel valued, they felt like the teachers didn't have faith in them. They see a whole different way of being treated and respected. … I wanted to make this a district initiative, so that no matter who is superintendent, the board members will say, 'We are a Kids at Hope *district*. Kids at Hope is here to stay.'"

On the other side of town, the Mesa YMCA takes pride in being the first in the country to apply the Little Kids at Hope model, which is designed for children age five and younger. The Y had been using the Kids at Hope belief system for older children in the after-school program for several years, and found it easy to incorporate it into the preschool program.

"The Y has core values—honesty, respect, caring, and responsibility—that we work into our daily conversation. To me, Little Kids at Hope, those core values, and the Golden Rule are all intertwined," says Joyce Chadwell, preschool director for the Mesa YMCA.

The children say the Kids at Hope pledge during morning circle, and even 18-month-olds do an impressive job of joining in the recitation that has become part of their routine. Teachers demonstrate their belief that all kids are capable of success by consistently praising children's efforts with high fives, stars and stickers, and verbal encouragement.

"For example, I was pointing to the letters of the alphabet, and one little guy named Sebastian could name every single one, and he got high fives and 'good for you!'" says Chadwell. "Then Christian said, 'I can do it, too!' but he went 'A, B, C, 1, 3, 10.' He got a high five and a 'good for you' too, because he did what he was capable of doing."

The preschool teachers read *The Kids at Hope Friends Visit Miss Debby's Class*, and use the plush dolls, Hillary Hope,

Oscar Optimism, and Sammy Success for an age-appropriate introduction to the concepts of hope, optimism, and success. Chadwell and her staff make a point of catching children in the act of being successful, and then acknowledging their actions with feedback like, "You were so kind to use those words with your friend," "Thank you for sharing that with me," and "I knew you could do it."

All 13 YMCAs in Phoenix have recently joined Mesa in incorporating the Little Kids at Hope model—reinforcing the city's reputation as a national leader in the belief that *every* child, at *every* age, is capable of success, No Exceptions.

The Right Time to Shift Focus
St. Lucie County

Community leaders in St. Lucie County were in the process of creating a gang prevention strategy to deal with their youth crime problem, when they heard about Kids at Hope.

"Our research included asking gang members why they joined gangs, and absence of hope came up as one of the top three reasons," says Christine Epps, executive director of the Roundtable of St. Lucie County, Inc. Shortly thereafter, Epps was at a conference where she picked up a book by Kids at Hope founder, Rick Miller. The book outlined the Kids at Hope research-based cultural belief system that states, "All children are capable of success, no exceptions."

"I thought, 'This is perfect!'" says Epps. "I bought 75 books and handed them out to roundtable members and others, including school board members and local politicians. When I went to get them back, everyone said, 'Oh, I gave it to someone else who I thought should read it, too.' … I have never seen something embraced so quickly with no negative comments or remarks. Our community was so ripe to want to make a shift in our culture. It was perfect timing."

Getting initial buy-in for Kids at Hope from the Roundtable, an organization of business, nonprofit, and service leaders, was the perfect starting point for a community-wide paradigm shift from "preventing crime" to "providing hope." Since the summer of 2008, more than 400 individuals who represent 79 schools, youth and faith-based organizations, and law enforcement agencies have been trained in the Kids at Hope model.

Denise Sirmons, supervisor of the Lincoln Park Community Center, has thrown herself into adopting the Kids at Hope belief system, which aligned perfectly with her existing approach to working with children.

"We were already sort of a Kids at Hope site without knowing it. It helps us be the Community Center we want to be, and need to be."

Children who attend the Center recite the pledge that says, *I am a Kid at Hope. I am talented, smart and capable of success. I have dreams for the future, and I will climb to reach those goals and dreams every day.* Sirmons created a recreation card that has the pledge on it, and it serves as a Community Center membership card.

"Kids love having the card, and showing it when they come in," she explains. "It lets them know they're part of this community. Before we had Kids at Hope in place, we may have had 15-20 kids a day. Now we have 60!"

She has also repurposed a wagon wheel into a Wheel of Hope that contains words that represent the areas from the pledge: goals, dreams, successes and talents. They've been taking it out to community events, where kids are invited to spin the wheel, and wherever it lands, they articulate that aspect of their future.

"At one event, we were the busiest place. Lots of kids came back for repeat spins, saying, 'I didn't tell you about my dreams yet!' She handed out beads with the Kids at Hope medallion to all the kids who spun the wheel, and says,

"They weren't so much excited about the prize as they were excited to tell us about themselves."

The Pace Center and the Garden City Early Learning Academy are also implementing Kids at Hope; and Epps reports that the Children's Services Council of St. Lucie County plans to train the 30-40 agencies they fund. The community hopes to expand Kids at Hope from Fort Pierce to Port St. Lucie by the end of 2010 and is applying for funding from the Children's Services Council to hire a part-time coordinator.

Community leaders have embraced the Kids at Hope model so strongly that when the Roundtable recently went through the process of reworking their mission and vision statements, the board members decided to incorporate the Kids at Hope messaging. They changed the vision from "an improved quality of life in St. Lucie County" to "We envision a community of opportunity where every child succeeds." The old mission, " To accomplish system change that results in improved outcomes for youth in our schools and in the community" became "To build a community that supports the success of children."

Those same community leaders understand Kids at Hope in action, as demonstrated by their participation in the Tunnel of Hope at Garden City Early Learning Academy. One of the Kids at Hope universal truths states, "children succeed when they are surrounded by adults who believe they can succeed, no exceptions," so on the first of school, the adults went to the school and greeted children as they walked through a Tunnel of Hope balloon arch. They called out, "We're so proud of you," "Welcome to the first grade," "We believe in you," and "We know you'll do well."

The following letter from a principal demonstrates how quickly and easily the Kids at Hope model effects positive change in children and ultimately—in a community.

"One little girl was angry, crying and refusing to go to class, as she wanted to stay in Kindergarten. As she exited the 'special welcome,' she turned to me and said, 'They said I was special and want me to go to first grade. I guess I can go to first grade.' She then went to class with a smile."

It Takes a Village
Herndon, VA

"I remember that within ten minutes of hearing the Kids at Hope philosophy, I thought this is what I want for my community—where I live, work, play, and raise my children," says Kelly Ginieczki, counselor at Clearview Elementary School.

"The term 'at risk' has been bothersome to me throughout my career. Kids at Hope uses scientific evidence to put 'at-risk' terminology to rest."

Over the past three years, Herndon garnered widespread support for the Kids at Hope philosophical framework that reverses the kids-at-risk paradigm and implements a belief system that says, "All kids are capable of success, No Exceptions." Thanks to a grassroots effort by committed volunteers, Herndon obtained a grant to become one of the country's first Hope Square Communities, defined as "a geographical location in which different youth organizations agree to share a common belief system and share resources so as to collectively be more effective than they can be individually."

Catherine Pressler, a culinary educator who's been a volunteer Kids at Hope Herndon organizer since the beginning, describes the range of local advocates.

"The Town Council adores what we do. The youth services officer from the police department is very supportive and so is the Parks and Recreation Department—they put the Kids at

Hope logo on T-shirts for *every* single program they run. ... State representative Tom Rust thinks it's very important, and here in Washington, D.C., having good political connections counts for a lot."

Clearview Elementary School has adopted the Kids at Hope model, which includes having the students recite the Kids at Hope pledge: *"I am a Kid at Hope. I am talented, smart, and capable of success. I have dreams for the future, and I will climb to reach those goals and dreams every day."*

"Our sixth grade does a schoolwide news show which is broadcast on classroom TVs at 2:30," Ginieczke explains. "All classes turn on the TVs and say the Pledge of Allegiance and then The Kids at Hope pledge. ... I have a lot of teachers who say, 'It really brings my purpose in teaching to the forefront when I listen to the kids recite the pledge.'"

One of the Kids at Hope universal truths states that "Children succeed when they are surrounded by adults who believe they can succeed, no exceptions." Ginieczki knows that the belief system is having the desired effect when she asks the students what it means to be a Kids at Hope School. One little girl recently replied, "At Clearview, every day I know I can learn something new. Here, my teacher tells me she will help me because she knows I can get better at reading."

Another universal truth says that, "Children succeed when they can articulate their future in four domains: home and family, education and career, community and service, and hobbies and recreation." Pressler describes community events, at which she gives children a chance to twirl a spinner that lands on goal, dream, career or talent.

"When it lands on career and you ask the children, many of whom are Hispanic, 'What do you want to be when you grow up?' they look stunned. They say 'A laborer,' as if there couldn't possibly be any other answer. When you suggest other things like, 'What about being a soccer player?' it is thrilling to watch the look on their faces as they begin to conceive of anything beyond being a laborer. I want to cry when I see that. These kids have never thought there was anything else."

In order to reverse the "kids-at-risk" paradigm, Kids at Hope needs to be a part of an overall culture and not just housed within the four walls of one school or organization. And that takes Treasure Hunters—caring adults who dig beneath the surface to discover the talents and intelligence that exist in all children, without exception. Herndon and Ginieczki, along with many other dedicated Herndon Treasure Hunters who have taken Kids at Hope to heart, continue tirelessly down the road of weaving a new way of thinking about children into the fabric of their community.

Spreading the Language of Hope
Hanover Park, IL

Anyone who walks into Anne Fox Elementary School can feel the positive Kids at Hope influence, but the school principal and the town mayor won't be satisfied until they're living in a Kids at Hope community.

When principal Nick Myers first heard about Kids at Hope, his school faced challenges, including significant disciplinary problems and toxic relationships between students and staff. Only 68% percent of students met state standards as measured by the Illinois Standards Achievement Test.

Four years later, every teacher and staff member, including custodians and secretaries, has been trained in the Kids at Hope belief system, which states that, "All children are capable of success, No Exceptions." Myers calls Kids at Hope the glue that holds all the positive outcomes together, and reports that relationships between students and staff are much more positive, disciplinary referrals are down, and that discouraging 68% figure has soared to 93%.

"If I left Ann Fox Elementary and went somewhere else, the *first* thing I would do is train the staff in Kids at Hope. You have to have that foundational belief before you can do anything else. Staff must accept no limits to the potential of the children with whom they work. If they lack this belief, we will fail children and lower our bar of expectation either intentionally or subconsciously. The Kids at Hope model really spoke to our teachers. It's a powerful framework, and it keeps them focused on why they got into teaching in the first place."

After implementing Kids at Hope in his school, Myers knew how important it was for others to reinforce that belief in his students' potential for success, and to understand how to put the Kids at Hope model into practice.

"We wanted our kids to be surrounded with Kids at Hope in the community. Kids have many shifts ... they may be at day care in the morning, and then at school, and then at a different day care in the afternoon before they go home. We wanted everyone who has our kids to know this belief system."

It was time to rally the town, so he wrote a proposal to become a Kids at Hope, Hope Square Community, spoke with a few local organizations, and ended up with 85 people from schools, the library, the mayor's office, and community organizations attending a one-day Kids at Hope training. He credits Mayor Rod Craig for much of the turnout.

"It was an eye opener," says Craig, of the training. "There were so many people in the room who were part of our educational community, and I thought, 'We have to get more government on board with this.' Craig has since become a vocal advocate for making Kids at Hope a community-wide initiative, and is working to get buy-in from the police and fire departments.

"You have teachers uplifting kids at school, but you have to have consistency with those messages at home and in the community," he says. "We need to get our arms around it and say this is our behavior in Hanover Park, and we're not going to accept anything less. When people start to see something like this that's different and consistent, the intrinsic value of the community goes up. People will say, 'I want to live there.'"

Myers has formed the Kids at Hope Hanover Park Community Coalition for the organizations that have already joined Anne Fox Elementary on the Kids at Hope bandwagon: Einstein Elementary School, the Community Resource Center, and the Hanover Park Park District. They meet regularly to talk about how they're implementing the model and the kind of progress they're making, which Myers says keeps Kids at Hope front and center. But he realizes that getting widespread community involvement isn't going to happen overnight.

"Here at the school, it's been easy to implement the Kids at Hope model. It made sense to the teachers, and it's been fun. Taking it into the community has been more challenging … but we keep working on it."

In the meantime, Myers sees daily evidence of Kids at Hope's positive impact. He speaks proudly of the fact that his secretary has her Four Aces cards, which define the important relationships adults need to develop with children, clipped to the bulletin board by her phone.

And he recalls one moment at an all-school meeting that captures what Kids at Hope means to each life it touches. They had asked a student from each grade level to read a portion of their Kids at Hope Passport to the Future to the whole school. One of the Kids at Hope universal truths states that children succeed when they can articulate their future, and the Passport is a tool that enables kids to describe and envision a future filled with hope, opportunity and success.

"This first grader named Rachel started reading her Passport about wanting to be a teacher, and her mother was just crying her eyes out. It was so powerful for all of use to see the students lay out what their future is going to look like, and to see how deeply touched that mother was."

All children need a champion, and according to Rod Craig, Hanover Park is fortunate to have Myers.

"Nick has my total, dedicated support. He has taken a school from the bottom to the top, and we are speaking in a different way in our community today. Kids at Hope is an example of how leaders of a community can help every child look at the world as a place of opportunity."

And in the not-too-distant future, Myers and Craig hope that all children in their community will benefit from the fact that everyone around them speaks the language of hope.

Meeting of the Minds
Lakewood, WA

Sometimes multiple sets of needs and plans intersect in a way that produces better, more far-reaching results than anyone could have hoped for. The Clover Park School District needed a new building for Lakeview Elementary School. The Boys and Girls Clubs had a plan to build community centers that would house a number of affiliated organizations. And Kids at Hope founder Rick Miller wanted to create Hope Square communities in which a school and the other organizations that serve their students agree to a set of principles and behaviors designed to ensure that every child in the community can succeed, without exception.

Numerous conversations and meetings among visionary child advocates led to a plan that united and benefited everyone. Local philanthropists Gary and Carol Milgard made a $10 million gift to build the Boys and Girls Clubs' first center on land owned by the school district. The school district launched plans to build a new facility for Lakeview Elementary adjacent to the Center. The result? The Lakewood Hope Square Campus that includes the Gary and Carol Milgard Hope Center and a new school that was renamed Lakeview Hope Academy.

"The Hope Square concept and the Boys and Girls Clubs concept of having centers that house a number of social services agencies meshed perfectly," says Wally Endicott, executive director of the Kids at Hope northwest regional office, which is located in the new Hope Center. "Every organization maintains its mission but shares the Kids at Hope belief system that all kids are capable of success."

The 31,000-square-foot Hope Center includes the Boys and Girls Club as well as dedicated space for agencies including Centro Latino, Child and Family Guidance, Lakewood Family Support, the Korean Women' Association, Safe Streets.

JoDee Owens, principal of Lakeview Hope Academy, not only made sure that all of her teachers and staff received the Kids at Hope training, but also created and facilitates a Campus Collaboration that includes representatives from organizations housed in the Hope Center, people from her school and from elsewhere in the school district.

"The whole purpose is to oversee that the Kids at Hope philosophy is well-grounded in the community, and to make it sustainable. At lot of times, organizations get together and get excited, but don't sustain it."

Two of the Kids at Hope Universal Truths state that, "Children succeed when they have meaningful and sustainable relationships with caring adults, and when they are surrounded by adults who believe they can succeed." Owens sees these truths at work at Lakewood Hope Academy every day.

"When you see a staff switch over to the belief that they matter to every single kid, it's phenomenal. You see every staff member talking to every child. They don't talk about 'my room' or 'my kids.' Now it's 'our kids.'"

Not only did the Milgard Family Foundation make the first Hope Center possible, but they further cemented the family's commitment to Kids at Hope by providing $250,000 in seed money to create the northwest regional office. Executive Director Wally Endicott has trained more than 800 people in the Kids at Hope belief system, including teachers, school bus drivers, nurses, kitchen helpers, youth services workers, and a group of fathers at McNeil Island Corrections Center.

"Training for this whole thing is imperative," Evans explains. "Everyone needs to hear it in the same way, and they need to buy in. We did a good job of spreading the word and getting people to come and learn about it."

Endicott works daily to identify and train more Treasure Hunters, defined as caring adults who search beneath the surface to find the talents and intelligence that exist in all children. He estimates that every day, 15,000 children in Pierce and Kitsap Counties have contact with people who are implementing the Kids at Hope model, but he sees many opportunities for additional outreach and says, "It really is grass roots. I'll do whatever it takes to move Kids at Hope forward."

And in the classroom, Owens sees that the children engage in positive self-talk by saying the Kids at Hope pledge daily: *I am a Kid at Hope. I am talented, smart and capable of success. I have dreams for the future and I will climb to reach those goals and dreams every day. All kids are capable of success, No Exceptions.*

"I've had kids who are in trouble because they've done something wrong come to me sobbing, 'I want to be a kid at hope. I want to be a success and go to college.' They've made a crummy choice and they're remorseful, and Kids at Hope gives them the language of hope."

And the Treasure Hunters who've made hope the official language of Lakewood Hope Square Campus continue to teach and promote fluency in the language that sets all of their children up for success.

When Opportunity Knocks
Chicago

When Teryl ann Rosch, executive director of the Chicago Education Alliance, first heard about Kids at Hope in the late nineties, she says, "I knew that somehow I would introduce the belief system into the schools. I just wasn't sure how I was going to do it."

Kids at Hope founder Rick Miller had gone to Chicago to talk with a number of people, including Rosch, about the belief system that reverses the kids-at-risk paradigm, focuses on strengths and opportunities, and sets kids up for success.

"When he started to talk about having high expectations for kids, that's what got my attention," says Rosch. "I said, 'You don't have to tell me any more.'"

She felt that hearing about Kids at Hope helped her identify the missing ingredient in a $30 million federal GEAR UP grant she had just submitted that outlined a way for universities to serve clusters of schools throughout the city.

"What had troubled me in all the focus groups we had was that there was alarming environmental pressure on teachers and principals who were dealing with troubled communities, and there was no belief system that kids were capable of moving through the system."

While continuing to work over the next several years to improve Chicago schools, Rosch became an advocate for the Kids at Hope model. In 2005, she wrote a third GEAR UP grant that introduced the Kids at Hope belief system, with a focus on training parents to implement it. Around that time, Rosch heard that the Chicago Teacher's Union and the Chicago Board of Education were forming instructional leadership teams to work with schools that were targeted for closing. Rosch knew the time was right, and moved to introduce the President of the Chicago Teachers Union to Kids at Hope.

She and several CTU representatives traveled to Phoenix and visited several schools that were implementing the Kids at Hope Model. The Chicago contingent was particularly impressed with the Kids at Hope Academy, a charter school for 4th through 8th graders who had been suspended from public schools and high school students who were not succeeding in traditional high schools. The Academy had been using the Kids at Hope cultural framework and practices for more than six years.

"They talked with teachers and principals, and it resonated that they were working with children who were having the same sorts of challenges that Fresh Start schools faced," says Rosch. "They saw data that after one year, kids who had talked about their futures with the bleakest interpretation were able to articulate their futures in a much more positive way. That was absolutely potent to the Chicago delegation. … They saw the importance of teacher buy-in and said, 'This is something the institutional leadership teams can adopt in the Fresh Start Schools.'"

In 2006, The Chicago Teachers Union received a grant to implement Kids at Hope in three of the Fresh Start schools, including Brian Piccolo Specialty School.

"I thought this is exactly what my school needs," says Amy Klimowski, Brian Piccolo's assistant principal. "When a school has been failing for 11-plus years, people lose hope … you're in such a state of despair. If you walked into the teacher's lounge you would hear things like, 'We'll be lucky if we can get two of our kids to pass.'"

Now, the teachers and staff embrace a belief system with Universal Truths that state, "Children succeed when they have meaningful, sustainable relationships with caring adults, and when they are surrounded by adults who believe they can succeed, without exception."

Another of the Universal Truths states that "Children succeed when they can articulate their future in four destination points: Home and Family, Education and Career, Community and Service, and Hobbies and Recreation." Every May, Klimowski and the staff do a Kids at Hope week, and on each day they celebrate how to be successful in one of the four destination points. For example, on career day, guest speakers talked about different careers; the teachers wore sweatshirts from their college alma maters; and the kids wore stickers that said, "Future ____" and filled in the blank with their planned career choice.

On the fifth day, they did an exercise related to the Four Aces, which are the four elements a child must have in order to succeed: the anchor parent, other caring adults, high expectations, and opportunities to succeed.

"Each child wrote a letter to someone who'd had a positive influence on them.," Klimowski explains. "We invited those people to an assembly, during which some of the children shared their letters aloud. One child wrote a letter to her foster mother, telling her she'd been a better mother to her than she could have imagined. Another wrote to a parent who was in jail. Needless to say, it was a very emotional time, and there were lots of tissues going around.

"Each year that we do Kids at Hope, it gets better. Our new principal came in and said [about the common belief system,] 'I've never seen anything like this!'"

So far, five Fresh Start schools have implemented the Kids at Hope model, and the Teachers Union recently assigned a full-time Kids at Hope coordinator for all ten schools.

"The chronic achievement gap arises in part from differing expectations that we have for more affluent student population than we do from low-income and minority students. Until we have high expectations for all kids, we're not going to see a narrowing of the achievement gaps," says Rosch. ..."I think that nationally, we're coming to a point where the whole social and emotional component of education is going to get more attention. The human side of the equation is going to be front and center."

Sometimes great ideas take hold immediately; sometimes they take a little longer. Today, dozens of Fresh Start students reap the benefits of seeds planted a decade ago, when Terry Rosch knew for sure that Kids at Hope would someday take root in Chicago schools.

John P. Carlos
August 4, 1943—April 25, 2004

Hundreds of audiences came away from John's presentations uttering their praise. "An amazing storyteller!" His poignant, humorous, powerful, and practical "storytelling" style wowed audiences around the world. Combining his business experience in the private and public sector, his stories were rich with human condition and powerful with applications that affected his clients' personal and professional lives.

John had the ability to draw you into his stories with humor and common sense. His talent for causing people to examine their own behavior first was a magnificent methodology for effecting change in organizational and personal lives. He had a unique ability to make people laugh while they learned.

John co-authored his first book with Ken Blanchard and Alan Randolph. *Empowerment Takes More Than A Minute*, immediately climbed to #7 on *Business Week*'s best-seller list. It has since gone on to sell over 400,000 copies in less than two years and is translated into 19 languages. This was followed by the equally successful *Three Keys to Empowerment.*

John Carlos was a senior consulting partner with The Ken Blanchard Companies, a full-service management training and consulting company with global headquarters in San Diego, California. His past experiences include director of training for the Circle K Corporation, 14 years as the executive director of various Boys and Girls Club of

America member agencies and several years running his own school, Celebration.

He was voted one of the Outstanding Young Men in America by the United States Chamber of Commerce and is a Vietnam-era veteran of the U.S. Army. John was a member of American Society of Training and Development, a member of the faculty of the American College of Physician Executives, and a graduate of the San Bernardino County Sheriff's Academy. He was awarded the "Key to the City of Indio, California" for outstanding community service and is a past president of the Running Springs Area Chamber of Commerce.

John received his bachelor's degree in business and a master's degree in business administration from Columbia Pacific University. John was a Life Member of the American Camping Association. He is survived by his wife of 35 years, Lynne, and has two daughters and four granddaughters.

Rick Miller

From the school house to the clubhouse and then on to the White House, Rick Miller has spent 40 years advocating, teaching, and supporting all America's children and youth.

In 1981, Rick served in The White House as a loaned executive in support of the President's Task Force on Private Sector Initiatives. Rick has also testified before congress on a number of issues affecting youth and the not-for-profit sector.

For 30 years, Rick was an executive with the Boys & Girls Clubs of America, including serving as the National Director for Government Relations.

In 1998, Rick was appointed Arizona State University's first Practitioner in Residence serving the Center for Leadership and Non Profit Management. ASU's College of Human Services recognized Rick in 2007 with their Visionary Award.

Rick founded Kids at Hope in 1999, a national initiative designed to change the paradigm from youth at risk to Kids at Hope.

Rick has published a number of influential articles on fund raising, organizational development, and youth services. Additionally, he has written two books, *From Youth at Risk to Kids at Hope: A journey into the belief system where all children are capable of success, No Exceptions!* and Kids at *Hope: Every Child Can Succeed, No Exceptions*, co-authored by international best-selling author John Carlos and foreword by Dr. Ken Blanchard of *The One Minute*

Manager fame. In addition to his Kids at Hope duties, Rick is on the faculty at Arizona State University.

Rick's breadth of understanding about youth development from a research, academic, and practitioner's perspective establishes his credentials as one of America's most informed and effective spokespersons for children. Rick is able to translate and bridge complicated theory into straightforward and powerful expressions about what is best for youth.

Rick crosses over all disciplines and is highly sought as a keynote speaker and presenter to academic, recreation, education, youth development, and law enforcement audiences all over the country. His wit, humor, and storytelling abilities captivate the imagination of his audiences leaving everyone who hears him believing that all children are truly capable of success. NO EXCEPTIONS!

Rick is a husband, father, and grandfather. He lives in Phoenix, Arizona.